DEFENDING THE
DIGITAL FRONTIER

DEFENDING THE DIGITAL FRONTIER

PRACTICAL SECURITY FOR MANAGEMENT

SECOND EDITION

Jan Babiak
John Butters
Mark W. Doll

WILEY

JOHN WILEY & SONS, INC.

Contents

List of Figures and Tables

Foreword

How important is digital security? Not very, if the scant attention that senior management has given it over the past forty years is any indication. And yet, suddenly everything is changing. Even Bill Gates is saying that digital security is *the* critical issue in business today. What is going on?

This book tells you. Ernst & Young has done a superb job of explaining why digital security is now at the very core of every business, and why protecting the integrity of the firm's digital information system must become a priority.

Computer viruses and worms may plague an enterprise, but these represent a mere fraction of the difficulties it faces. Computers can deal with objective, well-structured problems with amazing speed and detail, but they cannot cope with subjective subtlety, ambiguity, and complexity. Nuances of detail, as well as deliberate, accidental, and arbitrary actions feed back and continuously modify and amplify elements, processes, and subsystems that comprise the organisation. This mix of computerised information systems and human activity systems precipitates systemic risks: Unforeseen consequences—both hazards and opportunities—result, which are the product of feedback in the inevitable complexity of interactions implicit in all large systems.

A good technology platform, although necessary, is not sufficient for success. Success and failure are determined by unique social, political, organisational, and personal factors—not just functional ones. The real strategic difference for a firm is the added value that comes with understanding the way in which technology affects its various activity systems—the very topic that this book addresses.

From this perspective, it is clear that digital security is not just about computer crime and the like; it is a consideration of anything digital that compromises the integrity and well-being of the company. Companies must look beyond the functionality of digital technology, beyond the good intentions of the designers. They must look toward the observable, consequential hazards that occur when computers are integrated into society (in general) and into business (in particular).

As a result, the basis of digital security is *not* merely fiddling with cryptography, passwords, biometrics, profiling, closed-ciruit television (CCTV), and the like. Digital security must be broadly redefined as dealing with systemic risk. This strategic understanding of how technological and human activity systems interact, and the issue of maintaining the integrity of both, must pervade *every* aspect of management. It is fundamental to every successful business.

Nowhere is this understanding more evident than in the requirement for companies to comply with regulations. Despite new laws and regulations, most firms still find it very difficult to demonstrate that their computerised records are accurate, reliable, trustworthy, and secure. However, in an age of litigation this is crucial, and not just against instances of financial wrongdoing such as those seen in several recent high-profile cases. A firm—that is, its senior management—is held guilty until proven innocent by the production of all relevant data. The trouble is that no one knows which data is relevant until it is requested. The only sensible approach for the firm, then, is to keep it all!

Simply backing up this data as part of a disaster-recovery or business-continuity plan is not compliance. These processes usually involve discarding or overwriting back-up media well within the two- to three-year period demanded. It is not enough to rely on employees to preserve copies of their data and e-mail communications on their individual hard drives; these can easily be deleted, such as when the employee leaves the firm.

Unprepared managers, who are not able to prioritise among the blizzard of information emanating from their machines, find that the sheer scale and complexity of the data flow turns information into noise. Prioritising the flow of data requires "thinking managers" to have a clear understanding of the context on the basis of personal criteria, balancing the advice from a network of suppliers, colleagues, and customers. Only then can managers decide which approach is most appropriate to the complexity of their own situation. Exercising intelligent vigilance is paramount; this book proves very useful in teaching you how to do so.

Last, I should say something about a firm's board of directors. If they have not recognised the importance to the firm of digital security in the way Ernst & Young has defined it, then I have just one piece of advice for them: "Start the day with a smile and get it over with" (W.C. Fields), because they've got nothing to smile about.

PROFESSOR IAN ANGELL
LONDON SCHOOL OF ECONOMICS
AND POLITICAL SCIENCE

Preface

Throughout history people have been drawn to frontiers because of the potential rewards to be found there. But frontier life can be risky as well as rewarding. The pace of change in today's business world has propelled both the willing and the reluctant toward the digital frontier, where information technology (IT) has promised great rewards in increased productivity. But dependency on IT also exposes organisations to new and complex risks—risks that could seriously compromise reputation, undermine financial stability, or worse.

Unlike a physical frontier, this digital frontier is intangible and limited only by the imagination, which makes protecting it one of the most difficult challenges that businesses face. The challenge is heightened because digital security—the protection of *all* components of the digital frontier, including the human one—is complicated, costly, subject to judgment, and widely misunderstood.

Much of this misunderstanding stems from the belief among top managers that digital security is a technical issue, best left to the experts in the IT department. While many digital security solutions are technical ones, digital security is, at its heart, a management issue. Corporate leaders need to familiarise themselves with digital security issues as they would with any other major risk they face. Once they understand these issues they can shape the digital security agenda for their organisation.

To that end, this book is intended to be a practical explanation of digital security for executive management. It discusses the common problems of protecting information and provides a framework in which to analyse and discuss digital security. It offers independent insight into the organisational issues and processes that drive digital security and its supporting technology. The book then presents a set of mechanisms for identifying and managing commercial risk that is specific to an organisation's assets and people. It helps to separate the hype from the reality and gives managers the confidence to ask the right questions of their security experts.In a realm where the costs can sometimes outweigh the benefits, this book also helps ensure that information security budgets are spent in the most cost-effective manner.

This new edition takes a more global view than the first edition, which examined digital security issues from a largely American perspective. It is true that many American businesses arrived early at the digital frontier, but digital security is a truly global problem that many organisations, not only multinationals, must resolve, often across jurisdictions. These organisations not only need to coordinate their digital security planning globally; they must also deal with legislation that is sometimes contradictory on issues such as privacy. This new edition recognises and reflects these global challenges more explicitly than the first edition did.

As well as looking at digital security from a global perspective, this edition addresses the changes that the business world has experienced over the past two years. The most important of these has been an increased focus on corporate governance. Scandals at companies from Enron to Parmalat have caused stakeholders to place corporate responsibility for reporting under the microscope; all the negative publicity has put pressure on directors to take personal responsibility for their organisation's actions and behaviour. Governance around digital security has, so far, received less attention—but it is no less important. A high-profile corporate failure rooted in IT will no doubt focus stakeholders' attention on this important area. The fear of being considered the "electronic Parmalat," however, should be strong motivation for any executive management team to focus on digital security now.

Even if the challenges did not exist, the competitive pressures of the modern business world mean that many organisations have little choice but to live at the digital frontier. By doing so they gain many benefits but, to date, few have paid enough attention to the commercial impact of the risks they face. By tackling digital security as a management issue, and by strengthening their digital security culture from the top down, organisations can build secure and cost-effective futures at the digital frontier.

JAN BABIAK
October 2004

Acknowledgments

So many people have provided invaluable contributions to this book that it seems unfair to single out any for special thanks. We would like to take this opportunity to thank everyone for their contribution, whether technical content, business insight, research, or simply patience, support, and encouragement. We would like to extend special thanks to Daniel Lawrence for his editorial expertise and ability to express technical concepts in clear business language; Professor Ian Angell for his thought-provoking perspectives on information systems; Chris Reid of Tite & Lewis, Professor of Electronic Commerce at Queen Mary University of London, for his contribution on legislation; the Partners and staff of the UK practice for their technical and business insight; and many of the 3,000 Partners and staff of Ernst & Young's information security and technology practice worldwide for their international perspectives, in particular Edwin Bennett and Ed Napoleon. Our thanks go also to Sheila Upton, Simon Ash, and Rebecca Webster, who, with the authors, comprised our core team in the writing of this book, and Debra Englander and her team at John Wiley & Sons for their patience as we produced this second and global edition.

JAN BABIAK
JOHN BUTTERS
MARK W. DOLL

PART ONE

The Challenge of the Frontier

CHAPTER 1
Living at the Digital Frontier

CHAPTER 2
Security Characteristics

CHAPTER 3
Organisational Components and Security Objectives

T he desire to expand the bounds of knowledge has always led mankind to unknown frontiers. In the second half of the twentieth century, with the Earth well mapped, we left the protection of the atmosphere and opened a new frontier in outer space. The dawn of the space age coincided with the dawn of the information age. As space pioneers advanced from Sputnik to the space shuttle, global businesses started to explore the digital frontier by investing heavily in information technology and striving to reap the benefits of competitive advantage.

In many ways, the digital frontier is as unevenly explored as space. Some areas of information technology, such as mainframe security, are more likely to be well-established and the associated risks are better understood. Newer technologies, although heavily relied upon by organisations as part of a daily routine, contain inherent risks that are not as well understood.

A challenge that faces pioneers of both the space frontier and the digital frontier is preparing for risks that cannot be predicted or even imagined. Companies that want to reap the benefits of being at the digital frontier—increased productivity, market dominance, and increased customer satisfaction—must be prepared to defend their assets and their people against a variety of threats that may strike without warning. This may leave little recourse other than retrenchment.

Part One of this book describes the challenges facing executive management, whose decisions about how their organisations defend themselves at the digital frontier today, will produce effects that may be felt for years to come. Chapters 1 and 2 provide a discussion of how an organisation can determine where its digital frontier exists and an overview of the key characteristics of digital security. Chapter 3 addresses the issue of resource allocation including personnel, and provides a context for deploying the critical technologies, organisational enhancements, and necessary processes that will help an organisation in its pursuit of digital security. Together, these chapters present the foundation of a cyclical strategy to successfully defend an organisation's position at the digital frontier.

1

Living at the Digital Frontier

- Increasing Complexity
- The Digital Security Gap
- Mapping the Digital Frontier
- Challenges at the Frontier

The desire for increased profit and competitive advantage has always pushed business to adopt technological advances. Mechanisation, clipper ships, railroads, electricity, the telegraph, the telephone, computers, and the Internet have all brought step changes in productivity and efficiency that have led to improved bottom-line results. As the speed of technological advance, especially in information technology (IT), has increased in recent years, organisations have continued to take up the latest tools—whether or not they fully understood the associated risks.

This widespread use of IT has led to a sort of "digital frontier," a dynamic place where each organisation reaps the benefits of instant information access and increased productivity yet at the same time faces new and complex dangers. Some organisations choose to position their digital frontier at the "bleeding edge" of technology; they use the very newest, often still experimental technologies in speculative attempts to secure advantage over their competitors. Others take more conservative approaches, adopting new technology when the benefits and risks are more clearly understood. But no matter where an organisation chooses to establish its digital frontier, it must understand that there are risks and changes that need to be identified and managed at a senior level.

INCREASING COMPLEXITY

To understand how these risks have multiplied during the information age, it helps to trace briefly the history of the business world's use of IT and its increasing complexity. When organisations first started using computers, those computers were huge machines that took up their own vast rooms. The hardware, software, and operations were all housed in clearly identifiable facilities, and it was relatively easy to define what needed managing and who could access it.

With advances in processor power and miniaturisation, computers in the 1970s and 1980s moved out of the well-defined physical boundaries onto servers and desktops distributed throughout the organisation. The security risk was multiplied, but the networks were relatively simple; understanding what was connected to each network and how to manage it was relatively straightforward. The increasing complexity and reach of corporate networks however, brought a raft of new security challenges based around connectivity. These challenges increased as corporate networks came together in the biggest of all networks, the Internet, and linked to the networks of customers and suppliers. Compounding this, desktop machines were supplemented by laptops, notebooks, and personal digital assistants (PDAs), all of which moved out of the office and enabled employees to work anywhere, anytime (see Figure 1.1). The network is constantly changing, parties beyond the organisation's perimeters have access, and users control their own devices.

It has become increasingly challenging to understand what comprises security and who is responsible for it. With each step forward, flexibility and utility have increased, but so has complexity. In the 1970s, defending an organisation's IT infrastructure was not much more com-

FIGURE 1.1   Businesses' Usage of and Reliance on Information Technology (IT)

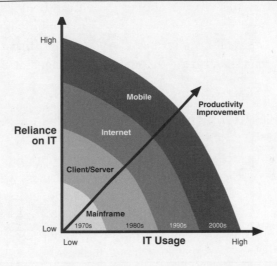

plicated than making sure the computer room had a good lock on the door. Today, a corporate network includes not only the machines physically wired together around different offices, but also thousands of devices connected over remote telephone lines, wireless fidelity (wi-fi) hotspots, and via Bluetooth connections or to mobile phone networks.

THE DIGITAL SECURITY GAP

As complexity increased and risks multiplied, few organisations properly considered the new risks they were taking on. Even fewer spent proportionally on mitigating these risks. This has created what we call the *digital security gap* (see Figure 1.2).

The challenges associated with the digital frontier must be identified, acknowledged, and managed for organisations to defend against them while maintaining their position at the frontier. Defending the digital frontier requires that organisations encourage an evolution within their security programmes. Detailed descriptions of this evolution are pre-

FIGURE 1.2   The Digital Security Gap

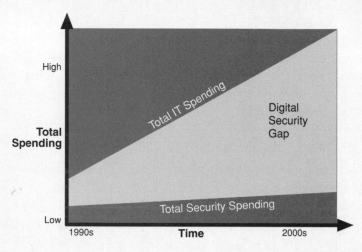

sented in Chapter 3 and Chapter 8. However, laying the foundation of this evolution is vitally important and is discussed in the following sections.

MAPPING THE DIGITAL FRONTIER

Meeting the dual challenges of remaining at the digital frontier while closing an organisation's digital security gap requires an understanding of what being at the digital frontier means to the organisation, as well as an awareness of how the organisation can defend its position there. It means executives must understand their organisation's own digital frontier and the associated risks their organisation faces.

An ***information asset*** is information of value to an organisation while conducting business. The information may be owned by the organisation—for example, customer lists—or it may be information placed under the custodianship of the organisation for a specified period of time—for example, a credit card number provided by a customer to complete a business transaction.

A **digital asset** is information stored or processed on or by digital media and the corresponding physical and logical devices used for storage, processing, or transport. Examples of digital assets include computer hardware and software, computer hard drives and the data stored on them, a network, and the range of a wireless hub. Digital assets must hold some level of value to stakeholders or be governed by a law or regulation to be classified as assets.

Eliminating all threats to an organisation's digital assets (and the vulnerabilities that affect them) is impossible as well as impractical, just as it is impossible and impractical to secure a nation's borders by building a perimeter so secure that it impedes the flow of commerce. However, securing digital assets is both possible and practical. Achieving digital security, much like achieving national security, becomes an exercise in identifying, mitigating, and tracking threats and vulnerabilities as well as repairing breaches. The work is cyclical and continual, and to engage in it effectively, executive management must know what information assets are at risk, the organisation's current digital security requirements, and its current digital security capabilities. Following a three-step process of assessing the environment, determining responsibilities, and setting priorities lays the foundation for a practical digital security programme.

Step One: Assessing the Environment

A broad understanding of the organisation's digital information assets and operations is required to determine where an organisation's frontier lies. This knowledge helps the organisation to identify and mitigate risk. Identification of this position involves much more than an organisation's simply knowing the usage of and reliance on its computing resources. Senior management must understand which assets to protect and why. For example:

- What are the operational, strategic, or financial issues or requirements driving the organisation's utilisation and reliance on digital technology?

- What are the capabilities of the current digital security programme?

An organisation's executive management needs to answer a number of questions such as:

- What information is worthy of protection?
- Which information requires greater or lesser level of protection?
- Where is the most important information stored?
- Is it clear which versions of the software are being used and are all the copies licensed?
- How quickly are patches assessed and applied?
- Is the software installed on one server or many? In which office or offices are the servers located?
- Who owns the database, and who determines who is allowed access to the data in it? How frequently are backups taken and where are those backups stored?

These are questions that the IT personnel in an organisation should be able to answer quickly. But do these IT specialists understand the value of the information? Should they? Should IT be the only repository of such information?

Organisations need to be able to identify their assets. This identification will involve the IT department certainly, but it is also an activity that must be understood and undertaken by management at the highest levels. Implementing every high-technology security precaution available cannot prevent unauthorised access to a sensitive database stored on a remote server if no one is aware that the server exists. This is why comprehensive asset identification must be addressed with rigour.

The next priority of the asset identification issue is to understand how an organisation's digital security requirements are determined. Is an organisation bound to comply with statutory regulations, including privacy regulations? Do business partners impose specific technical security configurations on an organisation's external networks? What would be the impact of an unintended release of sensitive or critical information?

The criticality and sensitivity of information assets may be—but are not necessarily—correlated.

Sensitive information assets are those that could, if compromised, pose grave threats to the organisation. Examples of sensitive information include unannounced strategic decisions, human resources information, or intellectual property, such as research and development data.

Critical information assets are those upon which the organisation relies to conduct routine business—for instance, to generate revenue and facilitate communications or transactions—and could include sensitive and nonsensitive information. An example of critical but nonsensitive information would be sales tax information for a retailer—information that is critical to running the business but is unlikely to compromise the organisation if released.

Every organisation has its own mix of regulatory-, industry-, and internally-driven digital security mandates; therefore, the answers to these questions are key to determining each organisation's digital security requirements.

Privacy is the right of an individual to determine to what degree he or she is willing to disclose personal or other information about him- or herself. When such information is provided to other entities, individuals, or organisations, this right extends to the collection, distribution, and storage of that information.

For today's global organisations, attempting to comply with different (sometimes contradictory) legislation and regulation in different jurisdictions can consume large amounts of time and resource.

Once the critical and/or sensitive information has been identified and the security mandates for protecting those assets are understood, the state of an organisation's existing security capabilities can be considered. What does that organisation's digital security programme look like today? For instance, how is the network monitored for unauthorised access? What is the process for providing new personnel with user access to Internet applications? What is the security configuration for the payroll application? Who has been given responsibility, direction, and authority to perform digital security functions? How much information resides on mobile laptops or palmtop devices and is it secured? Most importantly, could the models on which the answers are based be considered best-in-class, or even fit-for-purpose?

Step Two: Determining Responsibilities

For almost a decade, the Computer Security Institute (CSI) and the Federal Bureau of Investigation (FBI) have surveyed large U.S. corporations, government agencies, and financial, medical, and academic organisations about digital security. The results are published as the annual *CSI/FBI Computer Crime and Security Survey*.[1] One of the more chilling recent statistics presented in the survey is that 25 percent of respondents have suffered unauthorised access or misuse in the last 12 months to their World Wide Web site,[2] and out of this portion, 24 percent *did not know* if the incident had come internally or externally.[3] Other countries should not feel complacent. For example, in the United Kingdom, the 2004 DTI survey listed the "worst virus attacks" in 2003.[4] One statistic describes how 72 percent of UK businesses had received infected e-mails or files during 2003.[5] Yet a significant number of organisations update their antivirus software only infrequently.[6] The second step in identifying an organisation's security frontier is to *determine executive management's responsibilities* for defending the organisation's position at the digital frontier.

The overall objective of IT governance... is to understand the issues and the strategic importance of IT, so that the enterprise can sustain its operations and implement the strategies required to extend its activities into the future. IT governance aims at ensuring that expectations of IT are met and IT risks are mitigated.

—*Board Briefing on IT Governance, IT Governance Institute*

Management responsibilities for digital security are but one component of corporate responsibilities for IT governance. According to the

IT Governance Institute, which provides guidance on current and future issues pertaining to IT governance,[7] the responsibility for IT governance lies with the board of directors and executive management. Such governance "is an integral part of the enterprise governance and consists of the leadership and organisational structures and processes that ensure that the organisation's IT sustains and extends the organisation's strategies and objectives."[8] Specifically, with IT now so intrinsic and pervasive within enterprises, governance needs to pay special attention to IT, reviewing how strongly the enterprise relies on IT and how critical IT is for the execution of the business strategy.[9]

In today's global, digitally-linked marketplace, executive management has a fiduciary responsibility to shareholders and business partners as well as a responsibility to its organisation. The latter responsibility is operational in nature—to ensure the continuation of business in the face of threats and attacks. It is the responsibility of executive management to deploy a digital security programme that enables management to determine which risks to accept, which risks to mitigate, and which resources to deploy toward mitigation. Carrying out these responsibilities entails the following:

- Setting the objectives for digital security.
- Allocating resources for a programme to achieve and maintain digital security, including monitoring and measuring the programme itself.
- Promoting a digital security culture.
- Reducing the total risk of security failures while eliminating high-impact events.
- Conceiving a charter for the digital security programme that establishes goals and standards for an implementation framework.

Step Three: Setting Priorities

When an organisation's information systems fail publicly, for whatever reason, and whether the failure affects its networks, its Web site, or any other subsystem, more than just information is compromised: Trust is lost at every level and the corporate image suffers. The repercussions may be most strongly felt in regard to consumer confidence and, in turn, on the "bottom line." Therefore, the third step in facing the challenge of the digital frontier is to *define executive management's priorities* in defending an organisation's position at the frontier.

Earlier in this chapter, we referred to an organisation's digital security requirements and capabilities, and how best to identify digital information assets. Step three raises the same issues from a business perspective. For instance, what is the real threat to an organisation under or facing an attack? What will be the direct, immediate business impacts of a release of sensitive or critical information? Will all means of entry to the system have to be shut down? If so, for how long? What can be compromised in an attack—shareholder and consumer confidence, brand image, share price, or safety of personnel? What are the options with regard to defence? How fast is fast enough when responding to a breach of security? How much is enough to spend defending an organisation's position at the digital frontier?

Executive management's priorities are found in the answers to such questions. The challenge lies in determining what to do *before* a crisis strikes, and then doing it continuously. This means that the entire organisation must adopt a security mindset. It also requires executive managers to learn more than just the technical terminology of an organisation's digital security programme. They will need at least a basic understanding of what digital security means, what it involves, and what such a programme can and cannot achieve. Delegation of authority to those in the organisation who may not understand the business risk versus the business return is inappropriate and possibly dangerous.

There are many different responses to the questions raised in this chapter and they vary between organisations depending on the industry, the product or products produced, the organisation's reliance on technology, and the type of technology in use. Therefore, different organisations will have different priorities. The goal, however, should be the same—to build a digital security programme.

CHALLENGES AT THE FRONTIER

Information has always possessed an inherent value. Therefore, information security is not a new phenomenon. Evidence suggests that information protection is nearly as old as civilised society. Ancient Egyptians, Greeks, and Romans demonstrated varying degrees of expertise in encryption in an effort to keep sensitive information secret. Although the need to protect information remains the same, the methods of doing so have evolved rapidly in the information age.

Many traditional barriers to information exchange do not exist in today's business environment. Access to sensitive data no longer requires physical proximity. Data exists in smaller spaces and can be stored on increasingly compact, easily transportable media and can be transferred by wireless means. The benefits of speed and portability are balanced by the knowledge that information is more accessible and more difficult to protect than ever before.

Threats and Vulnerabilities

Once an organisation has identified its place at the digital frontier and executive management has defined its responsibilities and priorities for defending that place, it must determine the threats it faces and the vulnerabilities of its current security programme. Both threats and vulnerabilities if realised, can cause extreme damage, yet both can be effectively managed.

Five General Consequences of Threats and Vulnerabilities

1. *Interception:* Data is siphoned from the system.
2. *Interruption:* Networks, Internet access, or data stores are rendered unusable in a denial-of-service attack.
3. *Modification:* Authorisations, access codes, or data are changed.
4. *Fabrication:* False information is inserted into a system.
5. *Destruction:* Data is rendered unusable, for example, through a fire, flood, disintegration of old storage media, or other "acts of nature," or deliberate malicious act.

Threats to an information system arise from both human and nonhuman sources. Human threats can be divided into intentional and unintentional ones. Hackers, disgruntled employees, or others who have malicious motivation represent intentional threats. Those who damage systems accidentally—an employee who accidentally deletes important data, for example—are unintentional ones. Nonhuman threats include acts of nature that have no motivation yet could damage or destroy vast amounts of data.

Vulnerabilities are generally inherent weaknesses in an information system, although some vulnerabilities may result from deliberate acts or omissions. Despite quality control mechanisms, little commercial software reaches the market free from vulnerabilities, and systems developed in-house frequently suffer from the same problems. Potential avenues of attack are discovered almost daily, and such information is freely disseminated amongst the IT community and other interested parties, including potential intruders or hackers.

Common Causes of Information System Vulnerabilities

- Development efforts that focus on performance rather than security.
- A systems designer's inability to predict potential targets for exploitation.
- Inefficient change control.
- The average user's misperceptions of security risks.
- Misunderstandings about security protocols and the need for them.
- Developers under time pressure to deliver.

According to the 2003 CSI/FBI Survey, 92 percent of the survey's respondents had detected computer security breaches within the 12 months preceding the survey, and 75 percent acknowledged financial losses due to those breaches. The 47 percent of respondents that were willing or able to quantify their losses reported an aggregate $201 million worth of damage. The most serious areas of loss were the theft of proprietary information, which totalled $70 million, and denial of service, which totalled $65 million. The highest individual loss due to theft of proprietary information was $35 million; the average loss was

$2.7 million. The highest individual loss due to denial of service was $60 million; the average loss was $1.4 million. Insider abuse of Internet access—for example, employees' use of company computers or access to download pornography or pirated software, or the inappropriate use of the organisation's e-mail system—cost those who responded $11 million. Despite a high proportion of antivirus software implementation, viruses and their aftermath were detected by 82 percent of respondents and carried a price tag of $27 million.[10]

As this information shows, the risks are real and the stakes are high. All it takes is one person who doesn't "get it" to cause a security breach; that breach can take vast amounts of time, money, and manpower to fix and can have grave repercussions in the marketplace.

There are obstacles beyond threats and vulnerabilities that present challenges for organisations. Many of these obstacles are the product of misconceptions that permeate the decision cycle from the executive to the user level, and undermine security efforts. Examples of these misperceptions include:

- Information security efforts are an IT domain, or the responsibility of a specialised security group.
- Security threats and vulnerabilities are unique to high-profile industries or organisations.
- Outsiders compromise information most frequently, and such compromise is often detected and prosecuted.
- Security policies are sufficient to guide operations in a secure manner.
- Security technology will solve security needs.
- Security impairs organisational objectives and serves as a barrier to progress.

An Attack Scenario

Many threats exist on the digital frontier. Unfortunately, many organisations' digital security programmes are geared neither towards identifying these threats and addressing vulnerabilities nor responding appropriately to mitigate the impact of security incidents when such incidents occur. Consider the following real-world scenario and some of the questions it raises from the perspective of an executive who thought the organisation was secure.

Stage One: Onset and Initial Response

An employee who has been with a major healthcare services organisation for 15 years leaves the organisation under unfavorable circumstances. Shortly thereafter, her former coworkers and others complain that their passwords on certain corporate systems, such as e-mail, are no longer working. It is known that the ex-employee had knowledge of those systems, including default or known passwords, and there are indications that she has used that knowledge to access components of those systems. In an effort to resolve the situation, IT management issues an urgent request for employees to change their system passwords. Some employees respond as requested and change their passwords; others ignore the request. At this stage in the scenario, several issues have been raised:

- The organisation's policy regarding removing employees from the system when they leave is not being followed, nor is the organisation's policy regarding requiring employees to change passwords on a routine schedule.
- The organisation's policy regarding the use of corporate applications that rely on default or hard-coded passwords at the system level—in other words, critical application functionality will break if the passwords are changed—has been shown to be a vulnerability. There is apparently no policy restricting systems from using hard-coded passwords or requiring implementation teams to change default passwords prior to going live with systems.

The decision to shut down compromised systems or disconnect them from the Internet must be considered. Does current policy indicate the party responsible for making that decision, and does it address the impact of that decision on business?

Stage Two: Information-Gathering and Option Analysis

Because it appears the ex-employee has gained illicit access to the e-mail system, the potential exists that other Internet applications may also have been compromised, such as the organisation's online subscriber information database. Some of these applications may have default passwords that are crucial to their operations. The ex-employee may know these default passwords, or she may know other employees' passwords to these applications. As a response to this potential issue, programmers and vendors for the potentially compromised applications are contacted. They report that changing certain passwords on some systems is possible; however, it will take a month or more to make necessary programming changes and conduct remedial testing. The one-month time frame will affect the availability of the applications—perhaps even requiring that they be taken offline, which would necessitate a public explanation. This time frame will require adjusting the priorities of the current IT staff, thereby affecting the timeline of other projects currently underway.

Meanwhile, system and security administrators have put extra resources into the effort to determine how she is accessing Internet systems, but have little to show for their efforts. Some of the organisation's information systems are configured to log activity, others are not. However, even those systems that log information are only recording certain events, for example, failed logins. They offer nothing in this situation because the ex-employee is not failing to log in; she knows passwords and she knows the system's "back doors." She knows where the system's holes are, which means she could change security configurations on the system and no one would know. This raises the following additional issues:

- There are no implemented policies for logging security events on all systems or for accountability with regard to monitoring those systems.
- Without knowing which systems have been compromised, the organisation cannot learn whether data has been modified,

stolen, or deleted, or whether sensitive or critical information, such as customer data or information regarding business partners, has been compromised.

Stage Three: Escalation

Five days have elapsed since the first security breach was discovered. The ex-employee is still accessing corporate systems and changing employee passwords. She has hijacked the e-mail account of a current employee and uses it to send an internal e-mail to management. This e-mail, appearing to come from a current employee, complains that the ex-employee was "let go" unfairly and "did nothing wrong." The issues under discussion have become broader in tone, and more urgent:

- The decision is made to upgrade the situation from being an "incident" to a "crisis."
- The decision to contact law enforcement is considered, as well as the public relations ramifications of taking that step.

Stage Four: Malicious Escalation

The ex-employee sends another e-mail to selected organisation managers; this one contains an agenda. It reveals that for some time she was frustrated by the organisation's lack of security and that "no one listened" to her attempts to address it. Now she has their attention. The e-mail further reveals that she is in possession of patient healthcare histories and intends to disclose the information to the public, just to show how insecure the organisation's environment is. At this point the incident is upgraded in importance again, and activating the organisation's business continuity or disaster recovery plans becomes a consideration.

At this juncture, the scenario could move in several directions. However, the point has been made that the well-being of the organisation has been placed in jeopardy by the actions of one person who may have limited but critical knowledge of the system and perhaps only ordinary computer skills. This scenario or one eerily close to it could be played out in any large organisation in any industry at any given time.

Executive-level managers and corporate officers must ask themselves how it would be handled if this happened at their organisation:

- Would the digital security programme currently in place have the resources to find the necessary answers, and could it do so in a timely and organised fashion?
- Would prior decisions made by executive management about digital security empower or hinder those responsible for digital security as they sought to find solutions?
- What would it cost to address this scenario?
- What would shutting down a busy Web site for 24 hours cost in terms of lost revenue, not to mention the damage to the organisation's public image?
- What are the legal ramifications of having sensitive private information publicly released?
- What would it cost to have system administrators spend hundreds of hours investigating the incident and rebuilding compromised systems?
- What would it cost to have administrators and senior management spend dozens or hundreds of hours in meetings during and after the incident?
- What would it cost to have the public, government, and media relations departments spend hundreds of hours working on damage control plans and collateral materials intended to restore decreased customer and shareholder confidence?
- How much will the stock price drop, and how long will it take to rebound?
- What if such an attack happens again before the organisation has a new programme in place?

2

Security Characteristics

- Aligned
- Enterprise-Wide
- Continuous
- Proactive
- Validated
- Formal

The digital frontier continues to shift at a frenetic pace, forcing organisations to adapt continually to exploit the opportunities and address the challenges that come with change. An integral part of this environment is digital security that presents an organisation's management with decisions to be addressed to meet the specific needs of the organisation. Once management has identified its position at the digital security frontier, determined its responsibilities and priorities, and understood the commercial dangers of potential threats and vulnerabilities, its work has just begun. The next step is to design a model of an organisation in which the information assets can be secured to a recognised level, and then to determine how close to that model leaders want their organisation to be.

Constructing and implementing a digital security programme that meets management's definition of desired security practices entails coordination of efforts across the organisation.

FIGURE 2.1   The Six Characteristics of a Digital Security Programme

ALIGNED
ENTERPRISE-WIDE
CONTINUOUS
PROACTIVE
VALIDATED
FORMAL

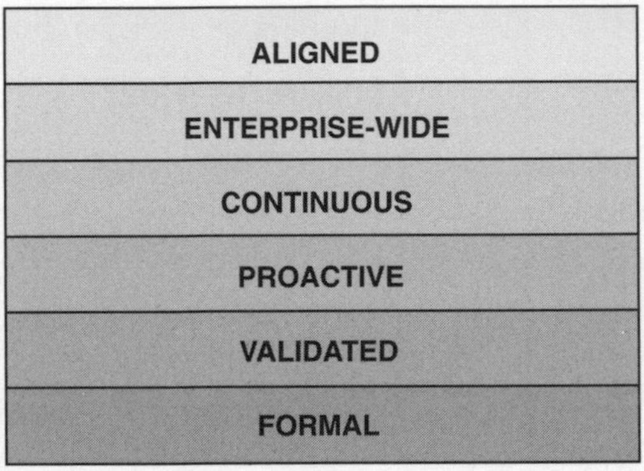

In this chapter we provide the foundation upon which an organisation can begin to plan and then construct a programme to achieve digital security. A strong programme consists of six characteristics that provide the framework for a fit-for-purpose security programme as shown in Figure 2.1. These characteristics can be built into the security systems. The goal is twofold: Maximise shareholder value by reducing risk at minimum cost and maximise return. Executive management can use the framework provided by these characteristics to determine how to approach the building of digital security into their business objectives. Throughout this chapter we make reference to the Ernst & Young 2004 Digital Security Survey, further details of which can be found in Appendix C.

ALIGNED

The optimal security solution for one organisation may look very different to the solution in a similar competitor organisation. But regardless of the differences, an organisation's digital security programme must be aligned to its individual business objectives. In order for management to arrive at a suitable solution for an organisation, it must attain and then maintain this alignment. Many organisations struggle to align digital security to business objectives for a number of reasons, such as:

- Justifying security expenditures within traditional return-on-investment models and need-based frameworks has always been difficult, leaving managers responsible for security decisions to make do with existing resources or expand resources in less critical but more visible areas.
- Decisions that should be made by business management are abdicated to the information technology (IT) department to make without sufficient business context.
- Management and the IT group do not work closely enough to ensure understanding of each other's perspective and priorities. Business management needs to understand the technical and wider elements of security, the technical threats to the organisation's security, and how best to use the options available to address business requirements. IT groups need to understand the business context and the impact of the technical options available.
- The core business units of the organisation and the IT group may view their objectives—for example, increased productivity and market share for the former and increased performance and security for the latter—as distinct from each other, rather than integrated. This lack of alignment can inhibit the IT group's ability to achieve its security objective, which is to enable the business units to achieve their objectives while protecting against loss or compromise of information assets.

In most large organisations, business objectives, such as increased productivity and increased market share, are supported by digital assets, such as customer lists, intellectual capital, supplier profiles, production schedules, and work flow. These digital assets are maintained and supported by the IT group, which traditionally also has responsibility for protecting them. The security function, however, is frequently relegated to a lower level on the organisational chart. The security manager might report to middle management within IT, security issues are blended into the larger IT picture, and the importance of the security function becomes diluted. The distance between the top levels of management and the security team, which is also the distance between the organisation's business goals and the IT group's protection of those goals, is known as the *security management gap*.

From the perspective of executive management, the security function is often a technical one, responsibility for which resides within the IT group. Decisions regarding security policies, practices, or technological improvements are frequently considered "wire and cable" issues and, therefore, best left to the experts, namely those on the technical side of the "security divide." Unfortunately, this delegation of authority places responsibility for important, even critical, strategic decisions—which will significantly affect the entire organisation's information systems—on someone who may not fully understand the organisation's business objectives.

Ignoring this lack of alignment is risky behaviour for any organisation because advances in technology continually compress the time needed to identify and respond to threats. It is incumbent upon top management to sponsor cross-business forums and to become directly involved in security-related policy and risk decisions by having a direct link to the security team. Risks to the business objectives and the possible impact of these risks must be determined by those at the top of the organisation. These same professionals must also set policy, after receiving expert input from digital security professionals and other operational and functional business leaders. Implementation, operation, and monitoring of security can then be delegated to the business leaders and the security team.

If, when an organisation is upgrading its technology, the executive management brings digital security into consideration, a security management gap would be less likely to develop. However, in the 1990s, extraordinary changes were taking place at the digital frontier and few senior-level managers understood the inherent risks associated with adopting the new Internet technologies. In the rush to implement new solutions, many ignored the good practices of systems development.

The focus was on improving productivity, and security was considered a secondary issue. These systems are still in use in the production environments of many organisations.

In summary, an aligned digital security programme is one in which executive management has recognised that digital security is a critical organisational element that enables the business units to maintain the productivity gains of the digital frontier. This recognition by executive management of the strategic importance of digital security manifests itself in the form of executive sponsorship. This means having direct accountability at the board-of-directors level, with dotted-line reporting relationships to executive steering committees, and the use of privacy officers. This visible sponsorship effectively places digital security high on the priority list of organisational objectives. When executive management exhibits this level of commitment to digital security, the security programme becomes aligned with management and business objectives. In an aligned situation, there is proper communication between the digital security team and cross-business executive management to ensure that pertinent issues relating to security are represented at executive levels in the organisation. The digital security team can convey information regarding the state of security in the organisation to executives and, at the same time, executive management can provide direct guidance to the digital security team.

> Twenty percent of survey respondents indicated their information security policies are reviewed for consistency with current business practices and risk strategies only when a perceived need arises.
>
> *Source:* Ernst & Young 2004 Digital Security Survey

The importance of aligning core business objectives with digital security decisions is presented in Figure 2.2. Highly effective digital security programmes are found in organisations that recognise the strategic value of attaining and maintaining a high degree of aligned protection for their information assets. Managers of digital security programmes within these organisations understand the direction established by executive management with regard to digital security policies. Therefore,

FIGURE 2.2 An Aligned Digital Security Framework

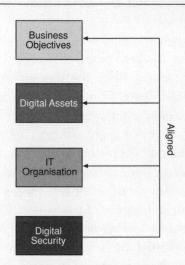

they can map those policies to the procedures and technologies that enable the programme to achieve its prescribed role, which is to provide the right level of protection for all of the organisation's digital assets.

As a final consideration under the alignment characteristic, the evolving regulatory environment in some countries finds many organisations with explicit responsibilities to provide external stakeholders with assurance that internal control over financial reporting is in place. Digital controls are fundamental building blocks of an effective internal control environment. Therefore, business and IT alignment over the digital security strategy and implementation is critical in these situations.

ENTERPRISE-WIDE

An organisation's digital security programme must be *enterprise-wide*. A successful programme takes a holistic view of the security needs for the entire organisation, as well as its extended enterprise; this enterprise includes customers and suppliers to ensure consistent, efficient deployment. A relatively low level of security at a low-risk division in an organisation may inadvertently undermine the security of higher-risk divisions. It is therefore important to understand the differences and determine a suitable approach to accommodate them. This alone is reason enough for executive management to pay close attention to the concept of enterprise-wide security measures.

Obstacles abound during the planning and implementation phases of deploying an enterprise-wide digital security programme, and any one of them can inhibit the programme's reach:

- Users and/or business management view security as an IT issue rather than an area with wider business considerations.
- Perhaps the organisation has a decentralised structure that has allowed several digital security teams to exist in different parts of the organisation, each with a different agenda and level of security expertise, and without a single point of coordination or direction.
- Digital security policies may not have been approved at an enterprise-wide level.
- There may not be anyone appointed with authority to mandate or implement enterprise-wide security.
- The lower-risk areas of the business object to paying for and operating security beyond their own requirements to meet the higher requirements of other parts of the organisation.
- Dependency on third parties or outsourcers.

Enterprise-wide digital security programmes share a common critical trait that enables performance at an enterprise level: *authority*. Such programmes are sponsored and funded at the executive level, driven by enterprise-wide requirements, directed by executive-approved policy, and are recognised across the enterprise as bearing the responsibility for carrying out digital security. These factors work together to establish the authority for the digital security team to operate an effective enterprise-wide digital security programme.

As Figure 2.3 shows, the concept of enterprise-wide digital security begins at the core of an organisation and moves outward in all directions, encompassing not only the organisation itself but the second and third generations of organisations on which it depends for secure sup-

FIGURE 2.3   An Enterprise-Wide Digital Security Framework

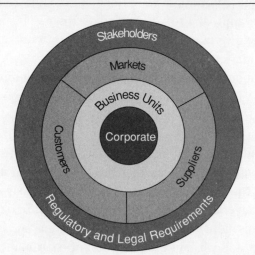

port and to which it must pledge to provide secure support. Enterprise-wide digital security moves outward from its initial core of the executive management team to include the organisation's business units. From there it expands to encompass:

- The organisation's markets, which include distributors, buyers, and sellers.
- The organisation's customers and those customers' customers.
- The organisation's suppliers and those suppliers' suppliers.

It extends further still to encompass other stakeholders in security strategies, such as regulatory bodies and national and local law enforcement. When taken together, these parts constitute a unified front for defence at the digital frontier.

CONTINUOUS

An organisation's digital security programme must be *continuous*. Real-time monitoring and updating of all security policies, procedures, and processes is critical to ensuring a timely response to issues and opportunities.

One of the difficulties of implementing a comprehensive digital security programme is that it must be *continuously* maintained. This presents an enormous challenge to any organisation, but it is particularly onerous to organisations whose executive management does not understand the commercial risks inherent in today's technology. In today's globally interconnected world, technology changes on a daily basis. Threats and vulnerabilities can appear and become full-fledged attacks within extremely compressed time frames. Much of the security technology changes in response to events or developments; preemptive changes are less common.

Inattention to security issues or inappropriate responses to security breaches place organisations at enormous risk of sustaining damage to their brand, their credibility, and their bottom line. Organisations should engage in a continuous cycle of assessing, updating, and redeploying their security programme. Such programmes adopt a *life cycle* perspective similar to software development life cycles, which incorporate steps from analysis to implementation. The digital security four-stage life cycle can be described as planning, architecture, operations, and monitoring as shown in Figure 2.4 and as described in Chapter 5.

FIGURE 2.4   A Continuous Digital Security Framework

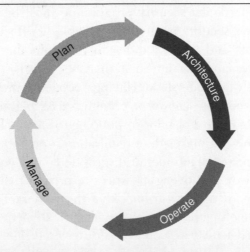

Executive management must coordinate the security objectives (maximal justified protection) with the business objectives (maximal performance utilising information assets). Once this parallel structure has been established and communicated to the digital security team, the programme must be developed and the assets secured. The secured state includes full implementation from a people, process, and technology perspective. As elements of the security programme are in place and functioning, they must be confirmed independently and as part of the larger system. New or unresolved issues (detected vulnerabilities, threats, procedural or organisational obstacles, etc.) must be addressed to restore full, secure functionality.

The next action taken is the most important, and that is to *initiate the cycle again.* Issues discovered during the confirmation process or changes made during the remediation process will have effected change within the overall programme and may have created new vulnerabilities. The digital frontier is continually moving; if the digital security framework does not continuously change to adapt to these changes it will rapidly become obsolete with potentially disastrous consequences.

PROACTIVE

An organisation's digital security programme must be *proactive.* It is imperative that a security programme be able to effectively anticipate potential threats and vulnerabilities to maintain the confidentiality, integrity, and availability of information assets. This is a substantial task that is frequently misunderstood. Having a proactive programme means taking steps to mitigate known or potential risks before they occur *as well as* having in place a plan for responding to an attack. It means paying attention to what makes the organisation a potential target, determining what a potential intruder or disgruntled employee might want to damage or destroy, and taking measures to protect those assets before an attack occurs. It means *learning* what the vulnerabilities are, monitoring the common paths of attack for illegitimate activity, and *curtailing* unauthorised activity as soon as it is discovered. The foundation of a proactive approach to digital security is ensuring that the organisation has applied sufficient resources to the digital security programme to enable these activities to take place; each of these activities requires research, planning, and monitoring.

> Only 12 percent of respondents have wide-scale deployment of vulnerability tracking mechanisms and knowledge of all critical information vulnerabilities.
>
> *Source:* Ernst & Young 2004 Digital Security Survey

To identify impending threats and vulnerabilities, those responsible for digital security must have access to multiple sources of information, both internal and external, and the time to review them. They must determine the validity or accuracy of the information. They must understand how the new threats and vulnerabilities could affect the organisation. They must synthesise the information and communicate it to executive management, and they must do all this quickly to be effective. If a digital security programme cannot support these activities in a time-effective manner, the organisation will be forced to operate in a reactive mode.

As shown in Figure 2.5, the traditional approach to digital security was to react to a real or potential threat by increasing organisational defences, only to allow the readiness to diminish as the threat faded. The next time a threat appeared, the effort required to address it effectively would be as great as it had been the previous time. That model was never cost-efficient; today, however, an organisation that allows its defences to languish because no threat is imminent could potentially be considered negligent. Today's threats appear more rapidly and are disseminated through globally-linked systems more quickly than ever before.

Organisations with highly effective digital security programmes understand the value of vulnerability management. These organisations dedicate resources to this effort and put in place processes that enable a proactive defence against new threats and vulnerabilities and ensure an appropriate response when they surface.

FIGURE 2.5   A Proactive Digital Security Framework

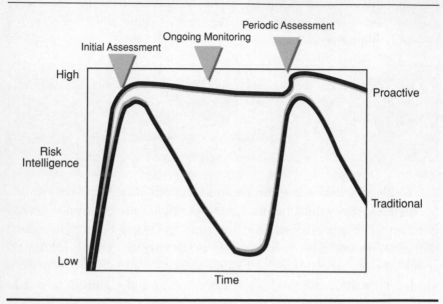

VALIDATED

An organisation's digital security programme must be *validated.* Achieving dependable digital security requires independent validation of critical security components. However, it also requires validation of business objectives. This dual, integrated validation effort enables an organisation to confirm that defined risk management and mitigation measures are in place.

> Seventy-seven percent of respondents indicated that their information security policies are not in complete compliance with the domains defined by ISO 17799, CISSP, Common Criteria, or other recognised models.
>
> *Source:* Ernst & Young 2004 Digital Security Survey

As mentioned in the discussions of the other key characteristics of a highly effective security programme, testing, or validation, is a vital step toward achieving full, effective implementation. The shaded areas in Figure 2.6 represent the need to balance, to some degree, the level of independence with the rigour of testing to achieve optimal validation results. For example, third-party validation may have limited value compared to that same third-party validation of a system to a given standard or business objective.

As shown in Figure 2.6, situational factors can dictate that internal testing is suitable—for instance, if there is a low risk of system failure and/or the impact of that failure presents a tolerable risk. If the system undergoing validation is at the business-unit level, self-testing, or testing by personnel responsible for the system or asset, may be acceptable. This is the minimum standard for testing. As the level of integration or involvement within the system or with regard to the asset increases, the risk of failure and/or the impact of that failure on the organisation increases, as does the need to mitigate risks. This situation must be addressed from a managed-risk approach, which renders unit testing

FIGURE 2.6 A Validated Digital Security Framework

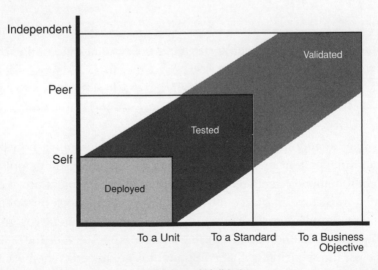

alone unacceptable but which may not necessitate independent, third-party validation. In such circumstances, it is possible that validation requirements can be met by having independent validation conducted internal to the organisation but external to the unit responsible for the system itself.

The third situation presented in Figure 2.6 involves the validation of trusted systems. When the unvalidated system is one that facilitates enterprise-wide productivity or performance, for instance, the e-mail system or critical data networks, the risk of failure increases dramatically as does the impact of that failure. In such a scenario, independent, third-party validation would be justified to ensure the enterprise-wide protection of digital assets at a highly effective level.

As Figure 2.6 illustrates, different levels and methods of validation apply to different components of a digital security system. However, whatever the level or method of validation used, there are two key principles that must be understood to effectively understand and utilise the results. The validation process must be thorough and repeated. A component or system is validated only at a fixed point in time, and changes to any part of the system may invalidate other components or subsystems in ways that are unknown.

> Over one-fifth of respondents stated that policy compliance is monitored or administrated in an ad hoc fashion.
>
> *Source:* Ernst & Young 2004 Digital Security Survey

Each component of an overall business process must be validated as an independent entity and as part of the larger system, application, or combination of technology that supports that business process. Validation must take into account interfaces or interactions between components, applications, and systems. As each component (or group of components that comprise a business process) undergoes the validation process, the security for that component is enhanced. When each component or group of components is validated cyclically, the security for the entire organisation is enhanced. The interval between validation efforts for each component, group of components, or business system will differ, as will the rigour of the validation process. This interval depends on several factors such as:

- The appetite for risk of the entity relative to each component.
- The maturity of the entity being validated. In the early implementation phase of any component or system, more security issues are likely to be detected. This requires more validation cycles than will be necessary when the component or system has been operating for a longer period of time.
- The number of areas of potential compromise within the component or system. If an organisation has 3,000 servers on 4 continents in 12 offices, testing all of them with any sort of regularity would be beyond the scope of most validation efforts. Therefore, the organisation may opt to validate small groups of randomly chosen servers according to a predetermined schedule.
- The quantity and type of resources available, not only to carry out the validation process, but also to follow through with remediation and revalidation.
- The rate of change in the security environment. The greater the rate of change, the shorter the validation cycle should be.

Where there is clear division between higher-risk and lower-risk components, the former may be validated more regularly than the latter.

Implementing a comprehensive, ongoing, tiered validation process that is based on a risk-directed framework will help enable an organisation to detect and manage vulnerabilities before they become liabilities, which is one more step to achieving fit-for-purpose security.

FORMAL

An organisation's digital security programme is likely to be more effective when it is *formal*. Policies, standards, and guidelines, which provide fundamental direction on digital security issues and are endorsed by senior staff, should be documented, tested, and then communicated to relevant members of the organisation.

It is important to note that for some organisations the testing and formal documentation of digital security and other IT controls have evolved beyond an important security characteristic. For example, documentation is a required aspect of internal controls over financial reporting for certain jurisdictions such as those regulated by the United States' Security and Exchange Commission under the Sarbanes-Oxley Act.[1] This explicitly includes information technology and therefore digital security.

Conceptually, a formal digital security programme seems simple and, in some respects, it may be. However, the designation *formal*, in this context, suggests that a programme possess a specific combination of qualities, as shown in Figure 2.7. The figure shows four classifications

FIGURE 2.7   A Formal Digital Security Framework

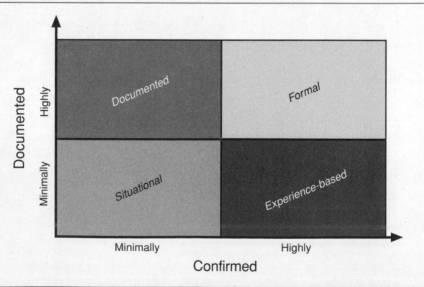

of a digital security programme: situational, experience-based, documented, and formal.

A situational programme is characterised by minimal documentation of policies, procedures, or processes, and minimal or sporadic confirmation.

For instance, when a virus is introduced to an organisation via a document that was edited on a home PC, digital security may isolate and remedy the problem. However, information about such breaches and precautions required to prevent recurrence are frequently not communicated to anyone outside IT. Policies or standards may not be updated to address the issue.

An experience-based programme relies on personnel—managers, IT or system administrators, or other persons immediately involved in the situation—to understand and resolve the issue and test the result. The confirmation effort is carried out thoroughly, the system is repaired, the organisation has resumed full operations, and the illusion of security is reinstated. Little, if anything, however, is documented. Furthermore, not much thought is given to what might happen if the same or a similar situation occurs when that person or department is unavailable.

A documented programme has all the paperwork completed, the policies in place, and the systems and components inventoried. However, when an event occurs, the entire system comes under suspicion because little, if anything, has been tested. No one knows if the system is configured according to policy, if everything is working properly, or indeed, working at all. When no one knows what is working, it is difficult to discover what is not working.

A formal programme requires the *documentation* and *confirmation* of technology, organisation, and process. The programme requires not only that policies and procedures are in place, but also that everyone in the organisation is informed about them. This means that the components and systems have been confirmed and that flaws and vulnerabilities have been identified, catalogued, remedied, and reconfirmed. When an event occurs, the organisation slips into crisis mode but does not succumb to chaos. The roles have been defined, the processes are understood, and the actions are initiated.

Eighty-three percent of respondents have a documented information security policy. Of those, only 25 percent reported that their policies are supported by documented procedures and guidelines that are implemented and followed.

Source: Ernst & Young 2004 Digital Security Survey

Digital security means much more than securing servers and keeping out hackers. It means assessing risk and then ensuring the organisation's digital assets are secure at every critical step of the business cycle and at every critical point in time. It means ensuring that executive management is not just informed of, but actively involved in the creation, implementation, and maintenance of digital security systems or programmes by streamlining the channels of communication between management and security teams.

Highly effective digital security can only be realised by an organisation when business and security objectives are aligned, when the focus on security is proactive in its approach and enterprise-wide in scope, and when the digital security programme includes formal processes to ensure that critical aspects are continuously maintained, updated, and validated.

Organisations that operate further away from the digital frontier because they have low usage of and reliance on digital technology face a proportionately lower probability of a security event and a correspondingly lower risk of impact from such an occurrence. As depicted in Figure 2.8, if an organisation has an informational Web site that is not connected to internal information systems, there is probably little reliance on the site for anything other than public relations. If it is hacked or defaced, it can be taken offline and recovered often without the event inflicting significant damage to the organisation. However, as also shown in Figure 2.8, as an organisation that deploys an e-commerce system increases its usage and reliance on digital technology and moves toward the forefront of technology, the probability of a security event

FIGURE 2.8   Technology Drives the Requirements for a Digital Security Programme

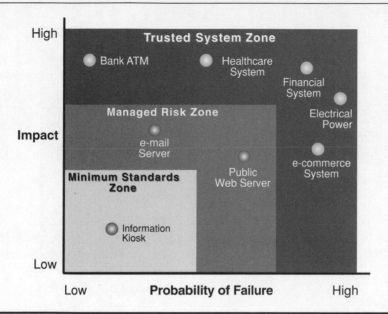

occurring increases—as does the impact of the damage from that event. This situation drives stricter security requirements. As Figure 2.9 shows, to meet those requirements, the digital security programme needs to exhibit the six characteristics outlined in this chapter to effectively manage risk.

As organisations have increased usage and reliance on technology, the stand-alone Web site has become an interactive tool used by customers and clients to place or check on orders, or to review private information. Although these enhancements increase productivity and performance, they also increase the organisation's risk of facing a serious security incident. Therefore, organisations have an increased need for security in terms of both scope and expertise. The organisation must move digital security from a reactive to a proactive state. Periodic digi-

FIGURE 2.9   Foundation of a Digital Security Programme

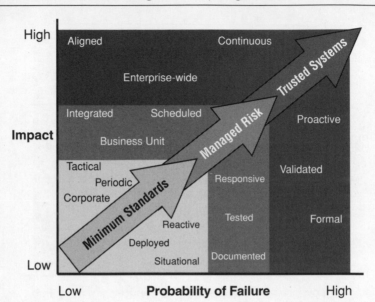

tal security must move to a continuous state. Each characteristic must improve over time. In essence, organisations have to move from applying minimal security standards to developing trusted systems. Before organisations moved toward the frontier, they might not have had pressing needs to have highly effective digital security programmes in place. They do now.

3

Organisational Components and Security Objectives

- **Organisational Components**
  - **People**
  - **Process**
  - **Technology**

- **Security Objectives**
  - **Confidentiality, Integrity, and Availability**
  - **Access Control**

- **Segregation of Duties**

Throughout Part One of this book, we have mapped the digital frontier, discussed its increasing complexity, and defined some of the challenges it presents including the identification of a "digital security gap." We have described some of the more significant threats and vulnerabilities and established the characteristics of an effective digital security programme. This chapter introduces the fundamental digital security objectives and the role of people, process, and technology in the operation of an effective digital security programme.

For success, a digital security programme must be effective, maintained, and balanced. The objectives of the programme must be clear and accurate, and the security procedures in place must ensure that those objectives are met. The programme must be balanced with regard to the expertise and leadership deployed at both the technical and managerial levels. There must be balance in the flow of communication

41

between those levels, especially for situations in which the business objectives and security objectives may not be completely integrated or understood. Those in executive management are most effective when they strive to achieve a balance between desired results and available resources; similarly, the digital security team is most effective when its members strive to achieve a balance between business, productivity, and asset protection.

The security environment is subject to continuous and rapid change. Measures that are effective today may not be sufficient tomorrow. Ongoing maintenance is essential to enable an organisation to adapt to these changes and remain effective. It is not just the threats that change; the building blocks of a security programme are dynamic as well. These building blocks are the people, processes, and technology of the organisation. As the programme evolves to meet new challenges, the parameters will also change because they are determined by the value that the organisation assigns to those building blocks (see Figure 3.1).

FIGURE 3.1   Organisational Components Support the Six Characteristics of a
Digital Security Programme

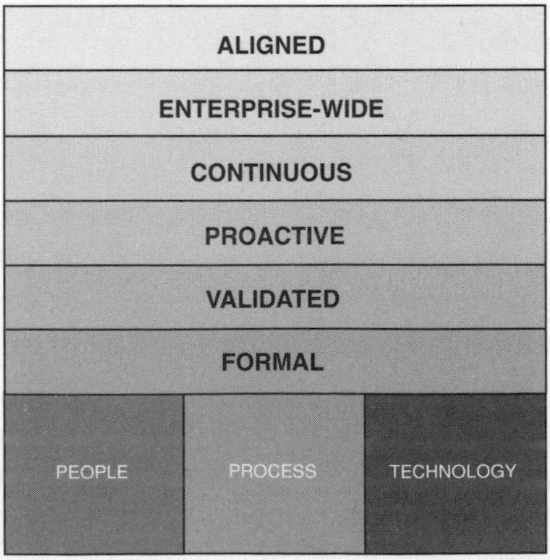

ORGANISATIONAL COMPONENTS

The success of a highly effective digital security programme depends on the value placed on three of the most important internal assets a business possesses: its people, its processes, and its technology (PPT). Deficiencies in any one of these can undermine the effectiveness of the entire programme, so organisations must make adjustments to ensure the ongoing balance and integration of these three building blocks (see Figure 3.2).

People

The criterion of *people* relates to the structure of a digital security organisation, the assignment of roles and responsibilities, and the skills and knowledge available. An organisation can deploy the best digital security technology available, but if its people component is weak, the digital security programme will fail to meet its objectives. For example,

FIGURE 3.2 Organisational Components

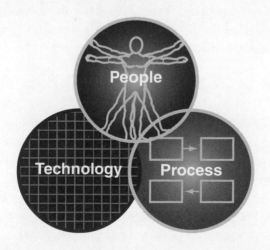

a software application that monitors systems 24 hours a day and sends warnings to the security staff alerting them to unauthorised attempts to gain access to the network would be helpful. However, if the right people are not available to receive and respond to the warnings in a timely fashion or are not trained in proper response countermeasures, the objectives of system monitoring cannot be met.

Highly effective digital security programmes invest in the people component of the programme. A formal structure must be established that clearly outlines authority and accountability and enables personnel to focus on securing the organisation's digital assets. Staffing must be adequate to fulfil the stated security objectives, and clear roles and responsibilities must be defined, documented, and understood. Staff directly responsible for information security must be experienced in security, technology, business, and communication issues; staff must also be familiar with potential scenarios of security threats or incidents. These skills must be fostered and continually developed to ensure that the programme keeps pace with technological and organisational requirements and can adapt quickly to situations as they arise.

People can often be the weakest link in security, so all staff, including contractors and temporary staff, need to receive relevant, ongoing education about information security and their roles in protecting the organisation. The investment in people extends well beyond the technology-based security team to all of the IT group, the end users, and business partners (including customers and suppliers).

Process

The *process* component of a digital security programme refers to the approved approaches or activities to be followed when operating all phases and aspects of the programme. These approaches or activities can range from determining how digital security policies are approved to how and when all personnel are trained in security-related issues to the steps to follow when a Web site is hacked or a system infiltrated. Having formal processes in place provides many benefits, among them ensuring that all actions taken will be within established policy boundaries and that people are prepared to take the right action when required, particularly in an emergency.

The process component for digital security is similar to its counterpart in a business unit. For example, expenses incurred by employees while conducting business may be reimbursable if certain policies and procedures have been followed and, in most cases, the reimbursement process is uneventful. The process was established to ensure that policy is followed, and that specific information—in this case, expenses—can be processed in an efficient manner. If a digital security programme is to operate consistently and effectively, repeatable procedures must be documented, understood, and executed. This includes procedures for initiating and implementing changes to existing policies and processes.

An established process for approving changes to security policies can mean the difference between a consistent, rapid approval cycle and a multiweek or even multimonth approval cycle. This time lag translates to having a digital security programme that can respond to a changing environment within a reasonable amount of time or one that cannot. Likewise, during an incident, having an established response procedure can mean the difference between losing customer information stored on one server and losing customer information stored on ten servers. Having an established response procedure can mean the difference between minimising the impact of an event and being unable to determine exactly which assets have been compromised.

Some organisations go a step beyond security training and implement programmes to validate policy compliance (this is in addition to any cyclical or ad hoc external/internal audit reviews). Although governments commonly employ this process, commercial entities are rapidly recognising the value of certification programmes. For example, if policies exist that require personnel in specific roles to have predefined skills or certifications, development or training efforts can be streamlined to match. The degree to which organisations develop and implement security policy is clearly an executive management decision that must be based on the aligned business and security objectives. Although recognised industry standards can be a good benchmark, they do not universally meet the needs of organisations. It takes time for organisations to develop, implement, and maintain a policy infrastructure that clearly supports their risk model and the accompanying technological infrastructure.

Technology

Poor processes and ineffective people cannot be fixed with technology. In fact, technology can take a poor process and can speed up or increase the damage caused by untrained people. Expertly deployed technology, coupled with trained, security-minded people and processes that are understood and followed, enables an organisation to realise significant productivity and security improvements.

The *technology* component of a digital security programme includes specialised software or tools focused on digital security, such as firewalls, public key infrastructure (PKI), user ID management, and an intrusion detection system (IDS). However, it also includes the planning for and configuration of other, platform-specific software or systems, such as Unix operating systems, hand-held mobile computers, and various types of routers. The technology components of digital security can include any hardware, software, or devices used to store or process digital assets or intellectual capital.

Like other technology components, digital security technology is commonly deployed to increase overall productivity. Furthermore, as with deploying and operating other technology components, adequate planning and design must take place to ensure that the investment is justified. This could include increasing or exceeding required service levels, reducing the effort and cost to achieve required service levels, or simply enabling the digital security programme to meet required service levels.

Today's globally interconnected world affords people with tremendous opportunities to share information; however, it also abounds with an ever-increasing number of threats to the integrity of organisational infrastructures. This situation presents tremendous technical challenges for increasing productivity while protecting digital assets. An executive officer understands that elements of each of the solution components—the people, the process, and the technology—must change to make an appreciable difference in the security of an organisation. If the people, the process, and/or the technology remain unchanged, improvements are unlikely.

SECURITY OBJECTIVES

Building the six characteristics of a highly effective digital security programme into the framework of an organisation's digital security structure requires an understanding of the fundamental tenets of digital security in technical terms, as well as in their application. As we have stated elsewhere, business objectives and security objectives must be aligned, and the goals of performance and productivity must be balanced according to those objectives. These concepts go to the heart of applied digital security: what the organisation's digital security programme must accomplish, and how it can go about doing this without undue interference in the core business agenda.

Confidentiality, Integrity, and Availability

Confidentiality, integrity, and availability (CIA) are the fundamental tenets of information protection and, therefore, of any digital security programme. *Confidentiality* assumes that data in its many states, including data in use, in transit, and at rest, is protected from compromise, including unauthorised access or disclosure. This includes the protection of data that does not exist; that is, when it has been deleted, it has been completely deleted. For example, when data is moved from a repository—a database, network, or even a hard drive—there must be safeguards in place to ensure that the reassignment or reclassification of that database, network, or hard drive will not subject digital information assets to compromise. Closely aligned with the concept of confidentiality, *integrity* assumes that data—in use, transit, or at rest and in any repository—is protected from unauthorised modification or deletion. *Availability* provides the counterbalancing assumption that data is and will remain accessible in required timescales by authorised users.

Although these objectives are central to the foundation of any digital security programme, they require implementation of people, processes, and technology if the objectives are to be achieved. The fundamental discipline in the attempt to achieve confidentiality of information is to control access to digital assets. This discipline is called *access control*. In addition to being fundamental to achieving information confidentiality, access controls play a major part in ensuring effectiveness of measures to protect the integrity and availability of information.

Access Control

In order for any system to function effectively, it must have in place the proper tools to issue permissions, grant entry, and verify identities. In the realm of digital security, however, it is especially critical to have such mechanisms in place. Determining the parameters of these mechanisms depends largely on the values held by the organisation and the value it places on its digital assets; the basic functions of the mechanisms, however, are the same. Achieving the optimum level of security requires that the system must be able to determine who is allowed to enter and what they are allowed to do; it must verify that the person using the system is indeed the authorised user; and it must perform these functions at every log-on and access attempt. The core methods used to control access are called *authentication* and *authorisation*; management of these methods is referred to as *administration*. These elements have a solid footing in the IT world as "the three As." We consider a fourth, less frequently discussed "A" to be just as important in deploying effective digital security: *auditing*. These four elements are discussed in the following paragraphs.

Authentication procedures involve establishing identity, that is, seeking evidence that a user is who he or she claims to be. Many security practitioners view authentication as the first line of defence for information systems. It is commonly held that users are authenticated in one or more of the following three factors: *knowledge* (something that you *know*, typically a password), *possession* (something that you *have*, for example, an access token or smartcard), and *identification* (something that you *are*, for example, fingerprints or retinal scan).

From a business perspective, authentication is arguably the most important of the three access control tools. If an organisation's digital assets are to be secured effectively, the security system must know who is in the system (with a reasonable to high degree of certainty) prior to that person gaining access to any nonpublic information. Knowing who is in the system facilitates tracking users' movements to determine where they are and what they are doing. Ultimately, the goal for access control schemes is to establish accountability; that is, every action on a system can be traced back to a single user or, in the case of automated procedures, a programme. For example, if an authorised user attempts to gain access to a system or asset prohibited to him or her, it could constitute a threat or it could be an innocent mistake. Either way, management requires a means of knowing who attempted to gain access. However, if authentication procedures are lax, or group authentications are allowed, management's ability to assess the action is limited; should the action be the precursor to an intrusion or an attack, there is little accountability and therefore little recourse.

Authorisation procedures involve assigning permissions to access specific digital assets. Once a user's identity has been confirmed, the system needs to determine what that user is entitled to do on the system. Common permissions include read, write, delete, or execute access. Such permissions may be based on any number of organisation-specific requirements, such as organisational role, need-to-know, or project-related status.

Determining appropriate authorisation privileges to information requires an understanding of the nature of the information to be accessed, the levels of access that different users should be allowed, and which specific users should have which defined levels of access. This is one of the primary areas of security that clearly belongs with business owners and should not be delegated to the IT group.

Administration involves the management of authentication credentials and authorisation privileges. It involves setting up, maintaining, and removing user accounts in accordance with the requirements defined in the authorisation process. While determining appropriate authorisation criteria is essentially the responsibility of the business, the responsibility for administration of access controls is frequently and properly delegated to a function in the IT department.

Effective administration can help resolve several key issues in digital security. One issue is the failure to revoke user privileges in a timely manner when employees leave the organisation or transfer within the organisation to different positions/projects that have different security profiles. In both cases, the employees or ex-employees retain authorised access to systems they should not be able to enter. Although authentication, authorisation, and administration are critical to attaining and maintaining access control, a digital security programme cannot be described as highly effective if no one is monitoring or auditing the system for failed authentication attempts or for authorised users who attempt unauthorised activities.

The *auditing* activities undertaken within the digital security programme should not be confused with activities undertaken during a financial audit. Auditing from a digital security programme perspective involves activities that assess the effectiveness of the people, processes, and technology that make up the digital security programme. Assessments are conducted to ensure that policy, procedures, and standards are implemented and followed, testing the real effectiveness of the digital security programme. The view that auditing is the fourth "A" of access control may not be widely held in the industry; auditing is therefore often addressed with less diligence or relegated to a lower priority than the other elements of access control. However, auditing helps ensure that authentication and authorisation controls remain effective and in place. For this reason, we consider it fundamental.

Systematically monitoring and reviewing system logs is the only way that system administrators will know who is in the system at any given time and what they are doing or trying to do; it is also the only way they will know when intruders are trying to gain access or if employees are trying to gain access to information they are not authorised to see. Mistakes in security configuration settings or an undiscovered vulnerability can leave a system exposed to unauthorised access. Because of the enormous volume of data generated by systems relating to user access and activity, monitoring this activity generally requires the assistance of tools and utility programmes, either provided as part of purchased systems or as add-ons.

Audit procedures involve continual evaluation of the output of various access control systems in search of unauthorised activities. When discovered, these unauthorised activities can be reported to management and the appropriate responses can be initiated. It is important to note that digital security auditing is not an activity that can be performed periodically; it requires continuous effort to achieve effective returns.

SEGREGATION OF DUTIES

A fundamental principle of access controls is the segregation of incompatible duties or functions. Certain combinations of access capabilities increase the opportunity for either fraudulent or accidental errors on a system; dividing these capabilities is a key measure that reduces this risk. For example, in most organisations the same people cannot purchase and authorise payments for goods. There are usually several different IT environments that should be segregated from one another, and within each there is often further segregation required. These are represented in Figure 3.3 and typically include:

- *Business users.* These are the various users of the organisation's systems for day-to-day business purposes. Their primary access privileges are to applications required to carry out their job functions. Business users should not be able to perform IT systems and administration functions or have the ability to make changes

FIGURE 3.3 Typical IT Environments

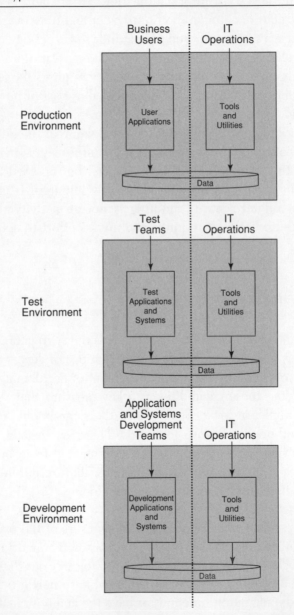

to production programmes. In addition, within this group of users there should be further segregation of duties to prevent individual users from having access to data or transactions that are not compatible with their business responsibilities.

- *The development environment.* This is where new systems or applications are developed or configured for future use in the business. To prevent programmers from implementing programmes that will not function as designed by the business, either through fraudulent intent or by accident, it is essential that this population of users is kept separate from other environments.

- *The test environment.* This is where test teams test new systems or applications before they are placed into production. The test teams are typically temporary groups made up of the intended future users of the system or application being tested; however, they should have separate user IDs and passwords to access the test environment to ensure effective segregation between test and production environments.

- *The IT production environment.* This includes all those responsible for operating and maintaining the IT infrastructure and applications. This covers a wide range of responsibilities including networks, applications, databases, security, and so on. The IT department should not have business user responsibilities or capabilities. Within this group there are invariably certain users whose activities are very difficult to restrict using conventional access controls, such as administrators of systems, applications, or databases. Other controls are required to help compensate for the inability to employ a "systems enforceable" segregation of duties, such as logging and monitoring these users' activities. Typically it is members of the IT operations group who have responsibility for moving data and applications between the different environments. In reality, these environments are likely to be logically rather than physically separated. See Figure 3.3.

- The framework for a highly effective digital security programme includes the components, organisational models, and objectives that populate its structure. When considered together, these fundamental elements form the foundation of a practical programme that enables an organisation to restrict access to digital assets appropriately, to run the programme effectively and achieve security objectives, and to recover when security events occur.

Part Two of this book provides an outline of specific items that an organisation can use to construct the environment of a digital security programme. By building on the framework suggested, this material provides constructive guidance on real-world security issues and provides end-state solutions that will help accomplish the objective of defending the digital frontier.

PART TWO

The Agenda for Action

CHAPTER 4
The Security Agenda

CHAPTER 5
The Security Life Cycle

W hile always exhilarating, exploring new frontiers has never been easy. Regardless of the era or their place in history, explorers are never complacent. Life on any frontier is fraught with uncertainties and dangers, but it holds an allure that the adventurous find difficult to ignore. Explorers at the edge of twentieth-century space exploration faced a daunting prospect. What lay before them held the potential for untold opportunity and success; it also held an equal potential for disaster. Business organisations at the edge of the digital frontier face a comparable challenge. Successful individuals in executive management not only exhibit the necessary determination to identify and develop opportunities, but also vigorously defend their ventures, not unlike the government leaders who sponsor space pro-grammes around the world.

Some threats to a twenty-first century organisation's digital security, such as viruses, can be expected. When they strike is not so much the issue as knowing that they will strike eventually and being prepared to respond quickly and appropriately when they do. Such threats occur with sufficient frequency worldwide that organisations with robust and comprehensive digital security programmes should be able to deflect or contain the virus attacks without reaching the crisis stage. However, latent threats and vulnerabilities exist as well and these are more difficult to prepare for. They may come in the form of malignant code that has not yet been triggered, invasive technology currently under development, or occurrences of catastrophic proportions that defy prediction. Organisations at the digital frontier must have measures in place that enable them to handle the unforeseen, the unpredictable, and even the unimaginable with reasoned response in a similar way to the more predictable virus or hacking attacks.

Part Two of this book provides a framework to help achieve such a level of digital security by designing a programme according to a structured security agenda. This agenda presents an enterprise-wide view of risk-mitigating items as well as a framework for discussion, action, and measurement of issues and responses. It outlines a digital security posture that relies on the interaction of people, processes, and technology to provide a fit-for-purpose defence of organisational digital assets. The security agenda addresses nine dimensions of an ongoing cycle of asset protection:

1. Defining and disseminating comprehensive policies, standards, and guidelines related to data and data protection.
2. Developing the ability to detect intrusions and viruses.
3. Implementing effective incident-response programmes.
4. Enacting privacy measures that allow the appropriate degrees of both transparency and protection.
5. Enhancing the physical security of components and infrastructure.
6. Implementing asset and service management strategies.
7. Determining and managing vulnerabilities.
8. Managing user access.
9. Ensuring business continuity during a crisis.

When an organisation facing the challenges of the digital frontier understands the importance of applying the key security characteristics outlined in Chapter 2 to the organisation's people, processes, and technology, as described in Chapter 3, it will have set the foundation of its digital defence posture.

The security agenda outlined in Chapters 4 and 5 presents a plan for building the superstructure of this posture. Chapter 4 focuses on the nine specific agenda items, while Chapter 5 describes how these agenda items can be deployed within a suitable security organisation and as part of an ongoing security process cycle of planning, designing, operating, and maintaining digital security.

4

The Security Agenda

- Policies, Standards, and Guidelines
- Intrusion and Virus Detection
- Incident Response
- Privacy
- Physical Security
- Asset and Service Management
- Vulnerability Management
- Entitlement Management
- Business Continuity Planning

A ny comprehensive digital security programme must satisfy three critical mandates:

1. It must enable the organisation to protect and monitor the confidentiality, integrity, and availability of systems and data.
2. It must provide this protection with the minimal disruption to the enterprise and, where possible, enhance the performance and productivity of the organisation.
3. It must enable the organisation to experience an attack, absorb the impact, and regain full functionality, all within a reasonable time.

This is where the principles discussed in Part One begin to move toward actions. To satisfy these three critical mandates, an organisation needs to create a security agenda. The security agenda is the platform

59

that the organisation uses to make a statement of principles a state of reality. Once created, the components of an organisation's security agenda provide tangible areas of focus for security activities.

It is important that the security activities are based on the security principles. To demonstrate, Figure 4.1 outlines nine specific security agenda components that support an organisation's objective to achieve a high level of digital security. The diagram illustrates that the six key characteristics, or principles, discussed in earlier chapters are woven into the security agenda or activities.

Throughout the remainder of this book we focus on these nine components which are common to most organisations, though they occupy varying levels of importance depending on evolving threats and vulnerabilities. However, to fit the needs of an organisation the security agenda components are likely to be expanded to reflect the environment, culture, industry, geography, changing threat landscape, and so on.

FIGURE 4.1   Digital Security[1]

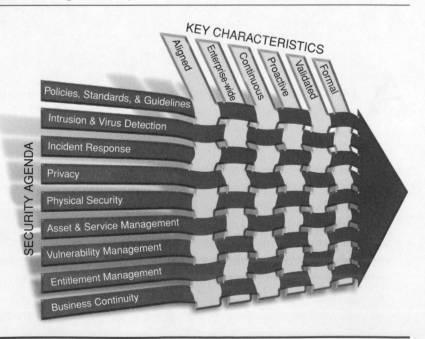

Subsequent chapters describe the capabilities for successfully implementing the nine components to appropriately restrict access to system resources, run the relevant processes and, where necessary, recover from significant security breaches.

Before we progress to an analysis of the nine components and the capabilities for a successful implementation, we need to briefly discuss the commercial drivers that are fundamental to the security agenda.

The foundation of a highly effective digital security programme is to ensure the confidentiality, integrity, and availability of digital assets by restricting access to those assets to authorised individuals and programmes only, and prohibiting access by others. Restricting access appropriately is a balancing act. If access is limited too severely, functionality is compromised; if access is not controlled tightly enough, security is compromised. This balance is the primary objective of security risk management.

There are other trade-offs to consider too, such as cost-effectiveness, intrusiveness, and time-to-market for new developments. In weighing the alternatives, a key goal is to achieve maximum security at an acceptable cost, in a manner that is as transparent and unobtrusive to the user as possible.

The primary focus of the security agenda is the prevention of security breaches, but because it is not feasible to eliminate risk completely, it is accepted that breaches will occur. The incident-response and business continuity security agenda items are designed to enable the organisation to detect and recover from breaches. Business continuity is responsible for creating an environment that supports the secure retention and recoverability of critical digital assets, and for identifying the people and processes that must be in place to ensure availability and continuity of key business systems and processes.

With this as background, we discuss the nine components of a security agenda in the context of the characteristics that describe a highly effective digital security programme: aligned, enterprise-wide, continuous, proactive, validated, and formal. These characteristics work together to form the core elements of the digital security programme by providing a technical architecture and framework of internal controls that enable an organisation to achieve highly effective, commercial digital security.

POLICIES, STANDARDS, AND GUIDELINES

Hackers' motivations vary but their basic approach does not: They find a vulnerability and they exploit it. An organisation may not know it is a target until it has become a victim, and this, in part, is why defending against an attack is so difficult.

An executive-sponsored and funded digital security team that is qualified and cross-functional is required to determine what needs to be defended and how best to institute an effective defence. The first step that this team must take is to put in place the policies, standards, and guidelines that enable an organisation to proactively plan, manage, and respond to information security risks, threats, and vulnerabilities.

The executive managers of organisations with digital security programmes in place understand that policy is the communication link between business operations and IT support. They also understand that formal rules of engagement that are documented, distributed, and implemented are essential to ensuring compliance by all of the organisation's personnel. The rules of engagement must include policies that are measurable, attainable, and supported by both configuration standards and behavioural guidelines. They define issues, roles, and responsibilities, effectively setting the bar for the digital security programme as a whole, and this clarity enables personnel to weigh risks as acceptable or unacceptable. Without formal, proactive, and comprehensive security documentation that instructs and guides behaviour and decisions, it is virtually impossible for an organisation to effectively manage and protect its digital resources. The three parts of this agenda item are further defined as follows:

- *Policies* define roles and responsibilities, state management direction, and provide for waiver documentation. How organisations determine domains of coverage for security policies is often as unique as their business model. Some choose to identify and conform to a recognised standard. Adherence to a recognised information security standard, such as International Standards Organisation (ISO) 17799, provides additional credibility for a security programme and may serve as a compliance goal for security practitioners. However, evaluation of whether such standards are aligned with the risk profile of the organisation should also take place to identify potential gaps or inefficiencies relative to the environment.

- *Standards* identify minimum security configurations for digital assets, are detailed, and typically focus on specific technologies and/or explicitly clarify vague policies.
- *Guidelines* provide direction to the organisation with respect to approaching digital security in specific situations or scenarios. Guidelines may be appropriate when there are more than one or two acceptable solutions for a particular digital security challenge, or they may evolve into specific policies, procedures, or standards as needed.

As presented in Figure 4.2, ensuring that an organisation's documentation suite is comprehensive and effective requires periodic reassessment and review, as does every functioning segment of a digital security system. Regulations and industry standards change, business practices and objectives are modified, the economy strengthens and

FIGURE 4.2 The Policies, Standards, and Guidelines Framework[2]

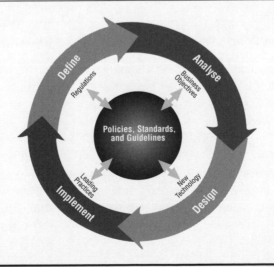

weakens cyclically, new malware (malicious code) and methods of digital attack are developed. All of these, as well as other events, can affect the suitability of an organisation's policies, standards, and guidelines programme. An organisation with a fully deployed programme of policies, standards, and guidelines is better equipped to adapt to such changes. The personnel required to carry out the update process are sponsored at the executive level. They understand both the organisation's business objectives and its risk with regard to digital security, as well as how policy modifications may affect those objectives. When the review and validation process is complete, the updated policies are communicated throughout the organisation in a timely and efficient manner.

Executive management must support the development and implementation of digital security policies, thereby establishing the charter for the digital security programme and lending it authority. Only with the unambiguous support of senior management can such a programme become effective, useful, and functional. Once it becomes functional, its value can be established and understood. Once senior management sponsorship is in place, policies need to be mapped to standards and guidelines, which are in turn applied by operations on a day-to-day basis and monitored regularly to provide assurance about compliance.

A Policy, Standards, and Guidelines Scenario

An organisation discovered that an employee was using the organisation's server in a test lab to download music files for personal use after hours. Although the employee had no malicious intent, he was unaware that his downloads were taking up network bandwidth and causing significant delays in testing a critical software package. The employee was reprimanded but not disciplined because the organisation had no formal policy that addressed the use of company equipment by employees for personal business. There were no guidelines for employees stating the implications of using company equipment for personal use or policies outlining the consequences for employees who abused company equipment or privileges.

The process of creating and formalising organisational policies, standards, and guidelines requires that organisations define their digital security posture and describe how the digital security programme will be implemented across the organisation. Organisations without formal digital security policies in place lack direction regarding their digital security posture and may lack the ability to defend their own position and/or hold employees accountable for their actions.

INTRUSION AND VIRUS DETECTION

The importance of knowing who is accessing an organisation's systems is a fundamental element of a digital security system. Knowing when people enter and exit a system, where they go and what they do while using a system, and whether they try to do something unusual or prohibited are valuable pieces of information. None of this can be known, however, if users' identities and permissions are not confirmed before they are allowed access to that system.

Knowing that everyone who accesses a system is there by invitation or permission is necessary because threats and vulnerabilities can appear with little warning. New software applications, new technologies, and changes to systems all carry inherent threats that can alter the stability or safety of an organisation's information systems. When systems administrators know who is accessing a system and have defined what is normal behaviour for that system, they are better able to determine when something is not right. They are also better able to determine if an anomaly should be elevated to the status of a potential security incident and forwarded to the incident-response team for investigation. A digital security programme must have comprehensive access control procedures and utilities in place. However, it must go well beyond this basic level of protection to prevent unauthorised or malicious intrusions where possible, and reduce the impact of intrusions and viruses when they occur. Various intrusion and virus detection techniques, such as gateway and content scanning, centralised logging, and antivirus programmes, can help reduce the risk of successful intrusion at points of entry and mitigate the consequences of intrusion events when they occur.

Intrusion and Virus Detection Techniques

Gateway scanning is a technique deployed to prevent unapproved or noncompliant attachments from entering a network or e-mail system by scanning the attachments.

Centralised logging is a technique deployed to facilitate the management of computer event logs. This technique involves systematically forwarding computer event logs to a single server, database, or system for analysis, storage, and management.

Antivirus programmes are software applications deployed to detect and remove malicious or problematic programmes or utilities (viruses) from a computer, network, or system.

Content scanning is a technique deployed to scan network traffic to detect Internet content that is not compliant with organisational policy.

Unauthorised or malicious intrusions and the dissemination of viruses can cause downtime, waste valuable resources for systems (and therefore personnel), and may cause damage or losses to sensitive, critical, or confidential data, cash, or other assets. Malware—viruses, worms, and trojans such as Nimda Code Red, NetSky, Bagle, MyDoom and SoBig—have shown not only how sophisticated cyber-threats have become, but also just how vulnerable large systems are to such insidious attacks. These can come in many forms and via many routes, and they wreak very different kinds of havoc on a system. The nature and number of threats "in the wild" are only two variables that make detecting, containing, and controlling the damage they inflict so difficult. Although the Code Red and Nimda attacks were costly for many companies, solutions were available. The most dangerous threat that any company faces is the one that it cannot contain or control. The speed at which intrusions are detected has a direct impact on the organisation's ability to contain and control them. The impact of other threats is a matter of degree, which correlates directly to the organisation's ability to deflect, contain, or control the threats or the impact.

Recent survey data indicates that external threats are a large cause of concern to organisations; however, external threats are actually less likely than threats that originate within the organisation. If the chance of sustaining an internal threat is greater than an external threat, traditional intrusion detection measures—such as firewalls, virtual private networks (VPNs), or enhanced physical security—may not be enough because the intruder is not an intruder at all but an authorised user. Highly effective intrusion and virus detection solutions can serve as indicators of imminent attack; these solutions can be used in conjunction with a solid security policy and incident-response programme to respond in near real-time to attacks in progress.

As shown in Figure 4.3, intrusion and virus detection is a central component of an aligned, proactive, and enterprise-wide digital security programme. A properly designed intrusion and virus detection system is not product-focused; it is programme-focused and employs many tools and techniques. It provides intrusion detection for all digital assets that could be targeted, such as the firewall, the router, the Web server, and the applications, and therefore functions as an early-warning tool. As

FIGURE 4.3 The Intrusion and Virus Detection Framework

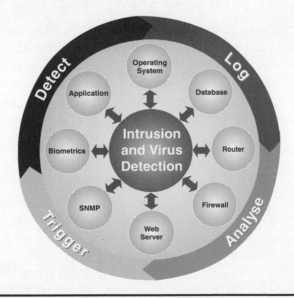

well as the technologies, people and process provide critical components of the intrusion detection programme.

Guidance on the people component—such as policies, training, and
certifications—and the process component—such as procedures, countermeasures, and standards—enables the organisation's digital security
team to detect, identify, and respond to intrusions, viruses, misuse, and
policy violations in near real-time. An intrusion and virus detection system
that takes such an approach (and is fully implemented) reduces downtime, mitigates real losses or damage, deflects damage done to intangible
assets (such as consumer confidence and corporate image), and maxi-
mises return on investment from security monitoring programmes.

Business requirements must be determined and used to justify the
deployment of intrusion and virus detection resources. The programme
should include education requirements that assist the design, operation,
and monitoring of the system as well as formal communication plans.
Once established, policies, requirements, and educational activities
should be routinely assessed and updated according to changing environmental conditions.

An Intrusion and Virus Detection Scenario

A global financial organisation had deployed their intrusion and virus
detection technology across several locations around the world. Sensor
systems were administered by regional personnel; however, there was no
central point within the organisation that collected and analysed alerts.
Late one evening, a computer worm began to infect several locations. The
worm stole password files from infected machines and sent them to sites
around the world. It also installed a distributed denial-of-service tool so
that the infected machines could be used in denial-of-service attacks
against other organisations. Since each site managed their own intrusion
detection sensors, information was slow to reach the Chief Information
Officer (CIO) and Director of IT Security. Before a decision could be made
to block all outbound network activity to contain the worm, infected
machines began to attack outside organisations. The event was reported
by the news media, and the financial organisation lost a significant
amount of revenue and market share based on the event.

> The distributed nature of digital environments demands polling and collection of network activity in a centralised, enterprise-wide fashion to facilitate control and containment of malicious network events that could significantly damage the organisation. Although in this scenario each intrusion detection sensor effectively performed its core function, the lack of aligned business and security objectives caused the digital security programme to fail. The lack of aggregation and centralised notification allowed the worm's malicious activity to compound its effect on the organisation.

One function of security systems architecture is to develop standards and guidelines for tools and processes required to operate effective intrusion and virus detection. Technical requirements are mapped to business requirements, and technical designs of automated solutions are developed. Should the technical solutions require third-party software or services, Requests For Proposal (RFPs) are developed and published. The operations team implements the solutions. Implementation includes the deployment of countermeasures, taking input from vulnerability management to guide overall response, and continuously updating the intrusion and virus detection systems to increase detection capability and capacity.

INCIDENT RESPONSE

Defining a security incident should be an easy thing to do. These days, everyone is familiar with the concept, if not the actions, of a hacker or a virus, and policy violations and denial-of-service attacks are fairly self-explanatory. There are lesser known but widely occurring incidents such as unauthorised use of networks or systems for processing or storing information, attempts to gain unauthorised access to data or systems, and unauthorised attempts to change or delete information within a system. Accidents and oversights cannot be ruled out either. New passwords are written down for the sake of convenience and are copied or stolen, an ex-employee retains access to systems after leaving the company, or sensitive or confidential data is erroneously posted to a Web site and causes financial or reputational damage. All of these scenarios, and many more, can be classified as security incidents and the response in each situation must be fast and effective to contain the incident, prevent escalation, mitigate the damage already caused, and lessen the costs of repair and recovery.

As mentioned in Chapter 1, the most dangerous issues within the realm of digital security are threats and vulnerabilities. Threats to information systems may come in the form of an attack. An attack is defined as *the exploitation of one or more vulnerabilities to cause the target system harm.* Information attacks most often serve as a means to an end and can be *active*, such as the introduction of a virus or worm, or *passive*, such as the interception of transmissions. The degree to which an attack succeeds is frequently in proportion to the opportunities afforded to adversaries by the targeted organisation. Organisations that fail to protect their resources present adversaries with unlimited opportunities for attacks; those that exercise security due diligence can diminish this window of opportunity.

A **threat** to an information system is any act upon or against the system that is performed with the intent of harming that system.

A **vulnerability** is an inherent weakness within an information system.

Active Attacks

Perhaps the most recognised active attack is the *denial-of-service* attack, which is an orchestrated effort to deny service to an authorised user by overtaxing the resources of the system, thereby rendering it unable to respond to requests for service. Engagement in a denial-of-service attack on a high-profile Web site is more often the means to an end rather than an end in itself. The desired outcome of such an attack may be decreased consumer confidence, public embarrassment, or diminished shareholder value. Potential adversaries who possess the requisite time, technology, and knowledge to orchestrate a denial-of-service attack need only to be willing to accept the subsequent risk of prosecution to successfully attack an organisation with malicious intent.

Existing protection mechanisms put in place by a targeted organisation may fail to prevent or compensate due to the distributed nature of such an attack. "Distributed" in this instance refers to the source of the attack, which can and frequently does originate from multiple users with or without the knowledge of the user, as described in the scenario presented in the section on intrusion and virus detection. Software code containing instructions to commence a synchronised attack can be disseminated in much the same way as a virus is disseminated, using automated propagation via e-mailed files, for instance. The code can reside benignly yet illicitly in a computer or a system unknown to the user or owner.

Denial-of-service attacks gained popularity in the late 1990s with high-profile successes against recognised e-commerce leaders, such as Yahoo! and eBay. According to the 2003 CSI/FBI survey, 42 percent of respondents had detected denial-of-service attacks in the previous 12 months, with an average loss of just under $1,500,000.[3] In addition to denial-of-service attacks, adversaries may engage in theft of service, software modification, or other types of active systems attack. These may include viruses (that replicate malicious instructions designed to be executed when triggered and that seek to infect information systems on a large scale), worms (malicious code that self-propagates through networks, causing damage along its path), or Trojan horses (programmes, scripts, or files that contain malicious code and are triggered after they have penetrated perimeter defences).

Passive Attacks

Passive attacks probably occur more frequently than active attacks, and the information gathered during a passive attack may fuel subsequent active attacks. However, passive attacks have an added element that makes them potentially more damaging than active attacks: An organisation may be under passive attack for extended periods of time without realising it because such activity produces little discernable data for systems administrators or security practitioners. (See the "Low and Slow" scenario in Chapter 7.) It is difficult to clearly estimate the percentage of passive attacks because the sheer volume of traffic on most networks precludes security, network, and systems administrators from collecting and analysing the data necessary to indicate passive attack activities on a network.

In many cases, passive attacks are used to capture information that may embarrass an organisation when made public. Passive attacks may take the form of *data interception*, or *sniffing*. This is accomplished through the use of a sniffer, a device that is used to assess network traffic. This is a widely accepted tool used by network and systems administrators for troubleshooting and for determining traffic flow. Its use becomes less benign when applied to nonoperational or unauthorised uses, such as to copy data as it passes a node on a network so that the data can be collected in order to monitor organisational communications, or to identify potentially exploitable, high-value targets.

Another utility widely used for routine and diagnostic purposes is *pinging*. This is a tool that sends a small message to a system to determine if the system is running. *Serial pinging*, which sends messages to many or all computers in a system within a highly compressed time frame, can effectively cause a network to lock up.

A highly effective digital security programme has in place continuous monitoring routines so that threats, vulnerabilities, and intrusions are detected. Without monitoring routines and policies that define a threat and provide instruction on how to proceed when encountering one, the entire organisation may be at risk or even under attack for extended periods of time. This can result in extensive damage in terms of diminished productivity, lost or compromised data, damaged or infected systems, corporate image, and consumer and shareholder confidence. In a worst-case scenario, the digital effectiveness of an entire organisation could be brought to a halt.

An effective digital security programme must have in place incident-response countermeasures that are understood by the entire enterprise and that have been practiced by the digital security team and allied personnel, such as systems and network administrators. A well-planned incident-response programme should ensure quick response, containment, and recovery times, and should include a multidisciplinary incident-response team operating within a phased incident-handling approach.

When a digital security programme is aligned with business objectives and it has made enterprise-wide awareness of incident-response countermeasures a priority, guidelines enable incident-response teams to be formed quickly according to the parameters of the incident. For example, an e-mail-borne virus attack that remains internal would require the expertise of security personnel as well as systems and network administrators. However, an attack or intrusion originating from a Web site may require a team composed of systems, network, and security experts, as well as Web server personnel, public or media relations personnel if the attack were made public, and legal personnel if crimes were committed. Incident-response teams should also be aware of assistance that can be obtained from external sources.

The purpose of an incident-response programme is to help protect and secure an organisation's critical assets when they are compromised while maintaining close alignment with one of the organisation's key business objectives: system availability. As shown in Figure 4.4, an

FIGURE 4.4 The Incident-Response Framework

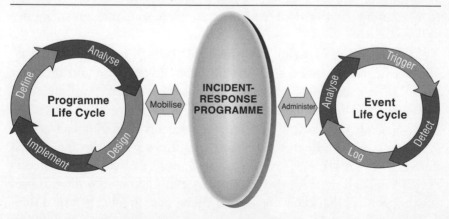

effective incident-response programme helps the organisation contain and recover from computer security breaches and threats by leveraging continuous event detection and analysis countermeasures; it also provides input to those who administer and define the tools and processes that enable protection, and does so in both reactive and proactive ways.

Functions that may be considered part of the incident-response programme include security awareness training, intrusion detection, documentation, and penetration testing. These proactive capabilities can help an organisation prevent computer security incidents while decreasing the response time involved when an incident occurs.

There are two major aspects of the incident-response programme: the event life cycle and the programme life cycle. The methodology of the programme life cycle is that programme objectives are defined, possible solutions are analysed, capabilities are identified, and the incident-response agenda item is designed and implemented. Administration of the agenda item indicates new objectives, which in turn drives the cycle to begin again.

The event life cycle is also continuous and plays out for every incident or event incurred. An event triggers the mobilisation process, which begins with detecting and logging the event. Analysis leads to decisions that enable control and containment. The analysis may also lead to the definition of new objectives, which in turn lead to alterations to the deployment strategy of the incident-response agenda item.

Assessing and absorbing the costs of damage inflicted during an attack is a painful process; bearing exorbitant response and recovery costs due to inadequate preparation adds insult to injury. A well-planned, proactive, and formal incident-response programme can reduce the clean-up costs of a security incident. An organisation with such a programme in place initiates preplanned routines when the incident is detected. Countermeasures to control damage and contain escalation commence, and recovery processes are set in motion according to pre-existing policies that allow nonsecurity personnel to quickly return their focus to core competencies.

The right programme reduces time and costs associated with incident response and recovery by analysing, upgrading, formalising, and validating response capabilities; providing consistent, repeatable methods and processes; and employing the leading technologies. It defines and implements tools and technologies that reduce the time required to analyse and respond to incidents. It also validates the organisation's current incident-response capabilities and formalises the appropriate incident-response processes and procedures necessary to align the programme with strategic business objectives.

Planning capabilities for incident response are key to initiating as well as maintaining a programme. Policies must be established that develop and maintain management direction and objectives. Policies that govern roles and responsibilities for incident response must also be developed. For example, it is through these executive-sponsored policies that production systems can be taken offline if such an action is deemed necessary to contain an incident. Business requirements for incident response are determined and used to justify the deployment of resources. Education requirements to execute the programme must be identified and provided to relevant personnel. Documentation procedures, which detail ongoing status and the value provided by incident response, must be established and distributed to relevant personnel for initiation and maintenance. All of these efforts are continuously reviewed and updated as conditions warrant.

A responsibility of security architecture is the development of standards and guidelines for incident-response tools and processes. Technical requirements are mapped to the business requirements and technical designs, and process flows of automated fixes are developed. RFPs are developed and published if technical solutions require third-party software or services.

The security operations function identifies and deploys the appropriate resources to contain the incident and mitigate any impacts. It then implements the systemic or incident-specific repairs and accompanying processes, assesses the health of the revised component or system, provides training and awareness, and conducts forensic investigations as appropriate.

An Incident-Response Scenario

A global manufacturing organisation had never fully developed a formal incident-response process and team. The organisation's IT group did not feel the need to expend time and resources in developing this kind of capability; they had never been "hacked" during their 27 years of operation. Then on a weekend afternoon in June, a hacker penetrated the organisation's network, stole password files, installed back doors, and downloaded confidential information about the company. Once the hacker obtained access to the internal network, his activities traversed the entire corporation across all geographical locations. As administrators were alerted around the United States and the Far East, the hacker began to divert his activities to other targets using the company's compromised systems as launching points. He left the organisation's network when he became aware that administrators were trying to track his activity.

Chaos and confusion marked the first 48 hours of the attack. Some administrators were not equipped to respond to the attack. Others, who were equipped to respond to compromised systems, did so in a variety of ways. The review and triage of log information was performed by several administrators independently, which meant senior management was unable to get an overall view of the state of security of the network, and the systems review procedures applied were inconsistent with established computer forensics procedures. Therefore, any potential evidence discovered would have been considered questionable in a court proceeding. The net result was that the incident cost the organisation several hundred thousand euros in remediation, and the hacker was never identified despite leaving numerous footprints of his activities on the network.

This incident is a classic study in how expensive complacency can be. By relying on history and statistical probability, the organisation chose to follow an ad hoc, reactive approach rather than a formal, proactive approach by not installing preventive systems across the enterprise. Because no formal communications structure or hierarchy existed and there was no validated reporting system in place, redundant and incomplete information was disseminated, which further hindered the recovery effort.

Malicious network activity often happens quickly, without warning, and puts company assets and brand at risk. It can also create the perception of lack of due diligence if the compromised network is used as a launching point to attack other organisations. Effective control and containment requires a formal, trained incident-response team that operates within distinct guidelines, follows accepted procedures, continually exercises its methodologies and updates them as necessary, and has the ability and authority to make time-sensitive decisions on behalf of the organisation. The alternative, a team formed on an ad hoc or as-needed basis, leads to an incomplete and ineffective response effort.

PRIVACY

Conducting business in today's connected economy means facing complex privacy issues that affect operations at all levels, including information systems. How an organisation chooses to address privacy determines whether its privacy policies are a competitive advantage or a potential risk. Business, technical, reputation, and regulatory risks associated with privacy must be determined. Organisations must balance these risks with the need to maximise the utility of the information they possess while building trust and confidence among stakeholders.

Because organisations now have the ability to collect vast amounts of data regarding individuals and limitless capacity to store it, developing, implementing, and maintaining privacy programmes have become highly debated issues in legislative forums and subsequently in boardrooms worldwide. The convenience of global interconnectivity has its risks, because dependence on digital systems increases the potential for successful penetrations of vulnerable or unsecured systems. Privacy concerns related to the gathering, storage, and use of information can affect organisations on many levels. Breaches of privacy—whether due to policies not being followed, intrusion incidents, or simply errors—can cause significant damage to image, brand, market share, and shareholder and consumer confidence.

Similarly, noncompliance with laws and regulations can initiate fines and, in some instances, failure to protect privacy can be legally actionable. It is critical, therefore, that executive management understand the risks of increased connectivity with regard to privacy issues. This is an incredibly challenging area. As organisations seek to standardise and consolidate global operations of information-related management, the laws applicable between countries can literally make the sharing of data within a company illegal.

This is a key reason why organisations with digital security programmes in place self-regulate their privacy initiatives, embrace third-party verification of their processes and technology, and have a formal privacy risk management programme sponsored at the executive level. Such programmes identify risks associated with privacy and help to ensure that the organisation's privacy countermeasures are conducted in accordance with fair information practices as well as within regulatory and legal guidelines. An organisation's privacy policies must address the entire enterprise, which, as defined in Chapter 2, includes business partners both upstream and downstream and the entities those partners entrust with critical information and organisational security.

A digital security programme must include an understanding of and commitment to privacy. It should include personnel responsible for identifying, interpreting, and applying new and existing laws and regulations that affect the organisation. It should have in place policies and procedures that drive compliance, as well as technical solutions that enable compliance. The policies must be documented and communicated to all departments and groups that work with covered information; policies must also be mapped to appropriate systems. If these basic safeguards are implemented, simply executing the digital security programme will keep privacy concerns in check.

Policies that address issues across the enterprise and at all levels must be developed, and management must take them into account when issuing decisions and directives regarding business objectives. For example, establishing World Wide Web-based database applications or interactive Web sites may require additional security precautions and countermeasures to ensure a higher level of user authentication. Roles and responsibilities on the individual and organisational level must be established and codified in policies as well.

Business requirements must drive the deployment of resources with regard to compliance with privacy requirements, for instance, the creation of an executive-level privacy officer. Risk assessments must be conducted to determine which digital assets may be in need of privacy controls. Once established, compliance should be routinely reviewed and appropriately updated, with incidents of noncompliance documented via a waiver framework.

The architecture team develops standards and guidelines for privacy-related tools and processes. Often, technical solutions provide the level of controls needed to ensure privacy compliance, for instance, on systems that are physically and logically disconnected from others. Business and technical requirements must be aligned and mapped, and technical designs of automated solutions developed. Any waivers should be analysed to determine whether solutions exist or extensions to the technical security architecture need to be developed. Ultimately, security architects are tasked to incorporate and apply technological solutions that lessen the chance that unauthorised persons will gain access to private information.

The operations team ensures that standards are deployed in accordance with the policies for keeping private information private, and for maintaining access privileges to restricted systems or areas. The operations team is also responsible for ensuring that such standards and policies are understood, implemented, and followed. This capability also entails continuous review of systems' status with respect to policies that ensure continued compliance as changes are made to laws around the world, as well as internal or industry requirements. Privacy training and awareness programmes are presented to ensure that employees understand the importance of privacy and know what tools are at their disposal for maintaining appropriate levels of privacy. Technical solutions that enable privacy protection must be in accordance with policy.

The monitoring team supports the operations team by ensuring that procedures for access to private information are followed, and that systems remain secure and are monitored for unauthorised use or transactions. These tasks include the following activities: conducting system audits, gathering information for compliance reporting, reviewing pertinent investigation outcomes, and if needed, assisting with any response to incidents concerning privacy.

Privacy Scenario

A leading cable company with millions of subscribers started collecting detailed information about its subscribers' Web surfing habits. When this became known, consumers, civil liberty groups, and privacy advocates became outraged and filed a lawsuit demanding monetary compensation for violations of privacy rights. Although only a subset of subscribers was being monitored, the cable company may face damages in the millions.

If the company had proactively created a privacy policy that clearly defined parameters for collecting and using subscriber information and formally communicated that policy throughout the enterprise, the business unit executive who made the decision to collect subscriber information would have been aware of the possible consequences and impact of that decision on the business objectives of the organisation. Had the same decision been made despite the policy directive, a validated and continuously monitored privacy programme would have alerted personnel that information was being collected in violation of the privacy policy.

Organisations are at risk on both sides of this issue. Litigation related to privacy issues is increasing at an exponential rate worldwide, and the monetary damages are substantial, resulting in higher insurance costs. On the other side of the issue, privacy-related regulations are constantly being modified and enhanced, making it imperative that an organisation's privacy programme be continuously monitored and upgraded to reflect those changes. Legislative changes and differences between individual country requirements present challenges that are not only for global organisations but any organisation engaged in cross-border activity. It is the responsibility of executive management to ensure that these privacy policies are clearly defined, communicated, followed, and monitored. For further information on laws and regulations, see Appendix A.

PHYSICAL SECURITY

Locks, bars, alarms, and uniformed guards are what many people associate with the concept of security. Such measures are fundamental to an organisation's total security effort because if the physical security of a facility or organisation is in doubt or in jeopardy, other efforts become significantly more difficult to initiate and deploy. When considering the framework of a digital security programme, physical security is often overlooked. However, it is a key component of controlling access to digital assets. Physical security efforts are often managed and directed parallel to, but not in conjunction with, the management and direction of digital security operations. This lack of proactive, enterprise-wide cohesion can lead to a situation in which the physical security measures that are intended to support the digital security programme are out of alignment with actual needs and requirements.

Protecting employees and company assets from unforeseen dangers and unpredictable occurrences is of increasing importance for senior management; physical security has become a fundamental component of overall corporate security. Appropriate building construction, adequate and consistent power supplies, reliable climate control, and effective protection from intruders are some of the issues that must be addressed when considering the security of buildings, infrastructure, and equipment, as well as of the information and systems contained therein. As organisations continue to seek digital solutions to increase productivity, one side effect has been the introduction of additional challenges to managing physical security. For example, the use of virtual private networks (VPNs) and wireless local area networks (LANs) has become more common in the workplace and larger numbers of employees are working from remote offices. As such, physical security plans must be adapted to account for more and more digital assets being operated outside the traditional, controlled, hardwired environment of the corporate office.

As shown in Figure 4.5, an aligned physical and digital security effort is coordinated at all levels and ensures that there are regularly scheduled communications between the digital security team and the .

FIGURE 4.5 The Physical Security Framework

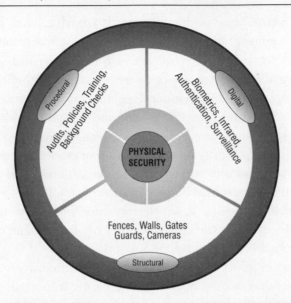

physical security team. The physical security team must have an understanding of digital security issues and adjust accordingly. For example, the use of automated systems for performing background checks or the introduction of digital surveillance or access control applications may require cooperative training between the teams. The physical security team plays a critical role in the execution of any disaster recovery and business continuity plans. Therefore it must be involved in their development and be a participant in corresponding exercises. Finally, regular testing of physical security controls that are in place can provide a benchmark and subsequently indicate how successfully the physical security programme is being executed.

Careful planning streamlines and enhances the integration of physical and digital security measures. Corporate security is most effective when the physical and logical flow of people, information, and materials through corporate facilities is understood holistically rather than as separate concerns and separate systems. Business goals and objectives and management concerns play a large role in developing policies that address physical security issues. Everything from the geographical location of offices to data centre security and hardware protection to offsite data storage facilities, as well as the responsibilities and obligations of individuals, must be taken into account when crafting such policies.

For example, organisations may need to educate employees across the enterprise as to the importance of clear-desk policies and screen-saver password policies. It may need to install locks for laptops or institute the use of removable, classified hard drives. Deployment of physical security resources must be in alignment with business requirements as well as actual needs. Such needs can only be determined by conducting risk assessments to determine which digital assets may be in need of physical security controls.

The architecture team can bridge the gap between the digital and the physical aspects of security. Standards and guidelines for implementing physical security policies must be developed. Technical solutions may be required to automate the implementation of some of the policies. For instance, if an organisation has determined that biometric countermeasures are needed to achieve the desired level of security, the architecture team is tasked with carrying out deployment. This includes determining which method best meets the organisational requirements—for instance, voice, retinal, or fingerprint recognition. It also includes determining the parameters of the system, purchasing and deploying the software and hardware, and configuring and validating the system.

The operations team must be closely aligned with physical security efforts to enforce the countermeasures that have been instituted to provide a secure environment for digital assets, such as handling situations when computers have been left accessible and unattended or media, such as floppy disks or CDs, have been left unsecured. The operations team also supports and carries out security awareness programmes and provides training for new systems and countermeasures.

The security monitoring function also supports an aligned physical security effort, particularly with regard to auditing aspects. Policies, standards, and guidelines include physical protection of digital assets, and the monitoring function is responsible for conducting audits to ensure compliance. Audits conducted to ensure that physical security policies are followed can identify gaps that may lead to strengthening policies, standards, and guidelines.

A Physical Security Scenario

A large university was the target of an attack by a disgruntled computer science student. The student manifested his anger with the university by entering the computer facility with a handful of magnetic filings, and disabling a mainframe that contained student records. Although the act was simple, it was extremely effective. Rather than risk exposing the backup tapes to the filings and suffering a total loss of the data, the decision was made to keep the systems down until replacement hardware could be found. Recovering this security breach took weeks of waiting for the equipment as well as hundreds of man-hours to repair and restore critical systems.

Even though access to the university's buildings and facilities was limited to students and staff, proper physical security countermeasures were not in place to prevent access to critical information systems. This "hard, crunchy outside and soft, chewy centre" is not uncommon among organisations that have yet to accept that threats exist internally as well as externally. This example underlines the importance of applying measures throughout the enterprise and not just at the perimeter to create a secure environment.

ASSET AND SERVICE MANAGEMENT

Productivity is a goal of almost any business organisation. Any mechanism, procedure, or technology that may improve productivity is typically assessed in terms of its potential utility and return on investment. The increasing costs and complexities of maintaining employee workspace have elevated the importance of implementing new methods of managing assets effectively and securely while improving productivity and accountability. These aligned objectives can be achieved by executing an integrated and comprehensive asset and service management programme, which may include help-desk functions, detailed asset repositories, change management processes, and self-service functions.

Asset management involves more than maintaining equipment inventories and software licensing documentation. It is a comprehensive approach to managing all of an organisation's assets: infrastructure, physical components, digital data, and intangibles. Assets that are overlooked or not accounted for can be problematic to the balance sheet in many ways. A laptop that is not accounted for (and thus not being maintained and upgraded with security patches) can become a breeding ground for vulnerabilities. For example, if the laptop has a connection to a rogue modem, it can be an entry point for an outside intruder, or it may have been compromised by a sleeper programme, which can be used to launch a future attack. The financial and reputational aftermath of such a situation can be significant.

Effective asset management in an enterprise must be sponsored at the executive level. It involves input from financial, information technology, procurement, human resources, and other areas in the organisation, including relevant third parties. It takes into account such things as lease management, order management, and asset tracking at the user level. Good asset management better enables organisations to understand their assets and the protection they require. When designed and implemented appropriately, an asset management programme incorporates the people, process, and technology drivers with a management process to provide clear information that enables an organisation to properly manage and track its assets, and the cost of those assets.

A well-designed and fully implemented asset and service management programme shows real benefits that can be measured in tangible terms. Efficiencies achieved across the enterprise include increased productivity for IT personnel and those relying on them, as well as reduced downtime of assets and improved customer service. Knowing what assets the organisation possesses, where they are, and who is accountable for them is essential for those tasked with effectively managing digital security. Also, this information contributes toward cost reductions and return on investment because tracked assets can be redeployed more quickly, resulting in less redundancy and enabling consolidation of maintenance contracts.

Planning for an asset and service management programme requires a detailed understanding of the existing work flows, authorisations, and integration as a precursor to crafting policies that support executive management-sponsored business objectives. Defining requirements for the future asset management process from procurement to retirement and understanding the digital assets that organisations deploy are essential to conducting comprehensive risk assessments; they are also necessary for establishing critical pieces of policy related to where those assets physically and logically reside and operate. Education programmes for individuals and groups responsible for assets, including those used off-site, must be developed.

The security architecture function works to create and maintain security standards and guidelines after determining what physical and technological assets must be protected. This requires an awareness of what technology is available, an understanding of how it will be deployed, and what it looks like from an enterprise perspective to ensure that the technical designs and systems architecture planned can scale to adequate levels.

After completing this technology survey, the architecture function designs the asset management system structure, building in the appropriate depth, breadth, and flexibility required by the organisation. This can include defining user and privilege profiles, constructing databases using appropriate and integrated software tools, determining naming conventions and data classifications, and constructing procedures for data migration. The architecture must provide security for assets at all levels and functions and enable enhanced business performance.

Security operations must have the capability to deploy and implement the formalised, established standards and guidelines developed for digital assets, and to continuously monitor those assets to maintain efficiency and consistency across the enterprise. This can include both manual and automated tasks such as setting up and maintaining user accounts, identifying assets as enduring or consumable, and ensuring that inventory control stickers are placed on appropriate assets.

Monitoring personnel must know the specific types of assets that are being monitored to understand where the sensitive or critical information resides and to better understand what activities are authorised or not authorised while conducting their monitoring. This capability supports the secure operations of an organisation by permitting hard assets to be tracked for inventory control and financial reasons. From a service management perspective, the monitoring team can leverage the capabilities of the organisation to coordinate communications and facilitate some aspects of digital security intrusion and virus detection.

An Asset and Service Management Scenario

During regularly scheduled maintenance of its digital assets, a major retailer discovered a potent virus resident in its systems. The virus was intended to deploy across the organisation's systems at a time of predicted high demand, and its payload would effectively destroy the functionality of every cash register. The virus was neutralised and a catastrophic event averted because of the integrated actions of the organisation's asset management and incident-response teams. The subsequent forensic investigation revealed that a disgruntled employee had deployed the virus.

Although the outcome of this incident was positive, the reality is that this situation could have been avoided entirely had there been a proactive, enterprise-wide digital security programme in place. Such a programme would have prevented unauthorised access by the employee into such a critical system. If the employee was authorised for that system, change control and monitoring applications would have issued alerts regarding system changes, and the insertion of the malware into the system would have triggered the intrusion and virus detection system.

VULNERABILITY MANAGEMENT

Thousands of vulnerabilities and associated exploitations are introduced into information systems each year. Disparate systems, platforms, and applications contribute to the difficulty of tracking new vulnerabilities and ensuring system integrity. Therefore, appropriate safeguards and potential points of failure must be addressed on an enterprise-wide level. A formal vulnerability management programme offers organisations an integrated solution that provides for consistent monitoring and automated methods of ensuring that compliance and secure configurations are maintained throughout the organisation. Taking this type of proactive approach can result in significant incident-response cost savings and an improved security posture.

An effective defence against unknown vulnerabilities can only be established when digital security decision-makers have a detailed understanding of the organisation's system and significant environmental threats and vulnerabilities. This information must be kept up to date and acted upon. Information about vulnerabilities and threats must be disseminated to the appropriate people, decisions made, precautions taken, and the results validated. Building accountability into the vulnerability management programme is key to its effectiveness.

Vulnerabilities within Information Systems

System vulnerabilities can include software bugs, which are inherent flaws in the code that cause systems to perform in unintended ways; unsecured ports of entry, such as Web servers; and back doors into systems, which allow or enable unauthorised activity. Physical vulnerabilities include unsecured printer locations or computer rooms; antiquated fire systems that unnecessarily damage equipment while responding to an incident; inadequate or unreliable backup systems; inadequate infrastructure controls, such as power backups and climate control; and inadequate offsite transport and storage practices.

The importance of having in place a vulnerability management programme is immediately apparent when one considers the estimated costs to global economies of recent malicious code attacks. Although these figures are typically the result of media sensationalism and are based on dubious estimates, they are evidence of enormous economic impact to the global economy and to individual organisations. Typically, these viruses exploited known system and code vulnerabilities, which means that much of the damage inflicted could have been prevented had the organisations known about the vulnerabilities and acted on that knowledge.

The vulnerability management agenda item is an enterprise-wide progression of protection that moves outward to expand the security of critical information and infrastructures. As progress is made and the programme is strengthened, the vulnerability management programme enables the organisation to track the status of vulnerabilities in real time by deploying appropriate controls, and to mitigate other vulnerabilities to the level of compliance with standards and regulations. Having in place broad, proactive methodologies to determine, deflect, and defuse security vulnerabilities means fewer incidents occur. Experiencing fewer incidents translates into less downtime, which means strong tangible and intangible returns on investment in a marketplace under near-continual digital threat.

The planning capabilities for a digital security programme rely heavily on the information contained within a vulnerability management system. Understanding vulnerabilities present in digital assets that organisations deploy is a prerequisite to crafting policies and conducting risk assessments. These tasks are critical to establishing programmes to educate the organisational population as to the importance of implementing and following behavioural and logical safeguards. Documentation procedures that detail ongoing status and waiver policies that detail the exceptions must be developed and distributed to appropriate personnel for initiation and maintenance. All of these efforts are continuously reviewed and updated as conditions warrant.

In designing a security architecture, it is essential to understand the nature of vulnerabilities that exist. In this way, an organisation can ensure that the technical design solutions created are adequate to protect current technological assets and the information they contain. Using policies already in place, an organisation creates security standards and guidelines for the vulnerability management system to specify how technology must be protected. Business and technical requirements must be aligned and mapped, and technical designs of automated solutions developed. Waivers should be analysed to determine whether solutions exist or extensions to the technical security architecture need to be developed. After the information-gathering phase has been completed, the team works to identify, design, and deploy technical solutions that support business objectives.

The security operations function implements the standards and guidelines developed for digital assets and continuously monitors those assets for configuration consistency. This is where the day-to-day vulnerability management takes place. Vulnerabilities identified for existing and new digital assets must be recognised, investigated, validated, and communicated across the programme to ensure that policies, standards, and guidelines drive the mitigation of risk associated with those vulnerabilities. In addition to exploiting technical system vulnerabilities, viruses and other malicious code infections in organisations typically involve the unintentional cooperation of end users, such as opening infected e-mail attachments. For this reason it is particularly important for effective vulnerability management that education and awareness programmes are implemented.

Monitoring personnel must know vulnerabilities that are both present (where risk has been accepted) as well as those that have been or should have been addressed. Information about the current state of vulnerabilities in the environment is crucial to everyday monitoring activities. For that reason, the organisation's monitoring capabilities must include appropriate levels of systems auditing to determine and support compliance and to assess changes in the vulnerability of organisational systems.

A Vulnerability Management Scenario

Viruses such as Code Red and Nimda exploited several known vulnerabilities that many organisations classified as low-priority and did not patch. Therefore, many organisations were unprepared for the viruses' ultimate impact. Organisations that had implemented a good vulnerability management programme and had evaluated the potential impact of leaving these vulnerabilities unchecked were able to apply to their assets the proper fixes to these vulnerabilities. In doing so, they eliminated many hours of unproductive time, resulting in potential savings of millions.

Vulnerabilities come from many different directions. Hardware and software manufacturers may issue patches to fix newly-discovered vulnerabilities in their systems. Many private and public organisations issue alerts and notices about vulnerabilities every day. Organisations need to understand these vulnerabilities, identify those that apply to their organisation, and develop a process to address these vulnerabilities in their environment. Any missed vulnerability can potentially expose an organisation to attack. Overlooking one low-priority vulnerability may not harm an organisation, but a combination of several such overlooked vulnerabilities could cripple it.

Without an effective digital security programme built around vulnerability management, organisations are more exposed to persons seeking to exploit vulnerabilities. A proactive vulnerability management programme can eliminate many hours of potential downtime, resulting in no or minimal interruption to the business.

ENTITLEMENT MANAGEMENT

Trust is a basic requirement in digital transactions. The customer or client must trust that the organisation will take appropriate measures to safeguard private information. Executive management must trust but also verify that the digital security personnel understand the importance of security measures from a business as well as technological perspective. The loss of trust can have a tremendous impact on an organisation's image and brand and, therefore, on its bottom line. Among the elements needed to establish trust in a digital environment is the use of the authorisation and authentication procedures introduced in Chapter 3. When such techniques are properly deployed, they provide a strong foundation for digital defence and trustworthiness of digital transactions. However, when poorly deployed, these techniques impart significant vulnerabilities to an organisation's IT systems, which can lead to exploitation, unauthorised access, lost data, unnecessary downtime, or other disruptions. Entitlement management is the security agenda item that addresses this critical element of digital security.

As seen in Figure 4.6, adequate access and permission controls affect many interrelated organisational systems. The need to effectively administer user access is critical to every level of a digital security programme. As an organisation's dependency on digital technology expands and the user base increases in many sectors—including employees, customers, suppliers, and business partners—the challenge of supporting cost-effective, secure user administration activities becomes greater as well. A standard framework for centrally directed entitlement management must be established and communicated to the organisation. A properly designed and deployed entitlement man-

FIGURE 4.6   The Entitlement Management Framework

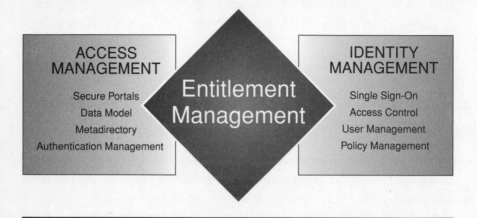

agement programme operates to control access to systems and to authenticate the identities of authorised users. These controls must be deployed enterprise-wide and must operate proactively and continuously to reduce vulnerabilities. Leading software companies are beginning to take an enterprise-wide view of entitlement management; see, for example, Computer Associates' Model of Enterprise Identity Framework, depicted in Figure 4.7.

The planning capabilities of a digital security programme set the direction for entitlement management and are key to initiating as well as maintaining the programme. Policies that address issues across the enterprise and at all levels must be developed, and executive management must take them into account when issuing decisions and directives regarding business objectives. For example, policies are crafted to ensure that user identities are authenticated accurately and user authorisations are applied and removed in accordance with other corporate policies. Roles and responsibilities at the individual and organisational level must be established and codified in formal policies as well. Business requirements must drive the deployment of resources, and risk

FIGURE 4.7   Computer Associates' Model of Enterprise Identity Framework

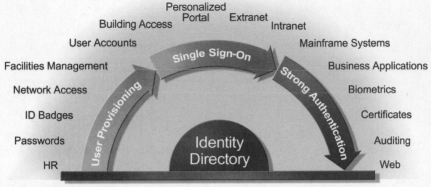

Source: Computer Associates. Used with permission.

assessments must be conducted to determine if certain digital assets may need more stringent controls. Education programmes must be established that effectively communicate both the policies and need for them to the corporate population. Compliance should be routinely reviewed and policies appropriately updated as business requirements change and technology advances.

As it works to identify, design, and deploy technical solutions, the architecture team must provide the leadership to ensure that the complexities of the technical architecture for entitlement management are integrated and scalable. Standards and guidelines must be developed that incorporate policy directives while supporting and enhancing business performance. Full functionality must be considered and tested prior to adoption.

The operations team often directs and administers the day-to-day entitlement management activities. Monitoring personnel are tasked with capturing user information and analysing it for unusual behaviour.

An Entitlement Management Scenario

Most organisations perform authentication based on an identification (called a user ID, sign-on ID, or log-on ID) and a password. As business functions grow, the assignments of these IDs and passwords grow as well. When a user of the business is assigned multiple IDs and passwords primarily because different technologies have different requirements for the way the IDs and passwords can be defined, they tend to forget the IDs and passwords and revert to the old way of doing things—they write them down. This exposes an organisation to potential compromise because these IDs and passwords can be easily obtained by others. Entitlement management provides a vehicle for organisations to define a single ID for a user across all business functions. Entitlement management also provides a way for organisations to productively guide the user through different functionalities of their business. This results in a more productive user, and it reduces the time involved in maintaining multiple IDs. Statistics also show that if an organisation does not manage user services effectively, they tend to lose potential customers to their competitors, resulting in reduced sales.

Authentication enables identity to be assigned to an individual within an organisation. Through authentication, trust is established. With this trust, organisations can authorise individuals to access digital assets. If this trust is violated, a user could cause significant damage to an organisation's digital assets.

Organisations need an enterprise-wide approach to entitlement management that proactively assesses the benefits of new and evolving technologies, and includes processes for regular revalidation of individuals' entitlements by business personnel.

BUSINESS CONTINUITY PLANNING

When describing core business systems, reliability and availability are not options; they are requirements fundamental to business survival.

When a disruption occurs, the organisation's ability to quickly and cost-effectively recover and restore critical systems, processes, and data is vital. Organisations must be able to rapidly deploy their people, processes, and technology to recover business operations and information systems during a crisis because digital threats can appear without warning and seriously compromise an unprepared organisation even before the incident has been detected. The losses in terms of downtime and damage to brand and corporate image can be significant. An organisation without a plan in place is an organisation that is either unwilling to consider the realities of digital threats to corporate security or unwilling to allocate appropriate resources to address the issue, and either situation is unacceptable in today's globally-interconnected economy.

The security agenda's final item, business continuity planning, presents a forward-looking, enterprise-wide approach that takes into account both organisational and technical issues when identifying the processes that are critical to an organisation's viability and success. Organisations with highly effective digital security programmes in place have well-developed plans that include formal emergency response teams, regular and frequent reviews, and comprehensive testing and training.

All aspects of digital security must be taken into account when constructing a business continuity plan. As shown in Figure 4.8, the busi-

FIGURE 4.8 The Business Continuity Framework[4]

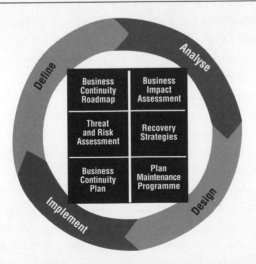

ness continuity agenda item is a four-phase process that addresses six specific issues:

1. Having a roadmap to define needs proactively.
2. Being able to perform business impact assessments that take into account aligned business and security objectives.
3. Having tested and validated recovery strategies in place.
4. Ensuring that the plan in place is updated and reviewed continuously, and therefore always ready for implementation.
5. Formalising the plan and distributing it to critical personnel.
6. Being able to conduct threat and risk assessments from an enterprise-wide perspective.

The planning team involved in business continuity efforts follows management directives to craft policies that guide the organisation through the chaos caused by any disaster scenario, whether digital in nature or otherwise. Policies may address the impact of topics such as the number of senior executives that may travel together or be present at the same location, natural disasters, or a full-scale, coordinated denial-of-service attack that brings down an organisational Web site. Risk assessments are conducted, governance methodologies are developed, and education programmes are established to inform personnel at all levels. All communications are formalised and distributed to appropriate personnel for review and implementation. Resources are directed according to business requirements.

The architecture team must develop standards and guidelines that enable systems to maintain or regain full functionality as quickly as possible after a disaster scenario occurs. This may include building extraordinary redundancies into systems in different locations or into backup arrangements, as well as other innovative, organisation-specific security precautions. Business and technical requirements must be aligned and mapped, and technical designs of automated solutions developed. Any waivers should be analysed to determine whether solutions exist or extensions to the technical security architecture need to be developed. RFPs are developed and published if technical solutions require third-party software or services.

A Business Continuity/Disaster Recovery Scenario

One week before Christmas, a truck backed into an electrical power pole in the shipping yard of a major distributor of groceries and supplies to restaurants, hospitals, nursing homes, and grocery stores. The damaged power cable shorted out all communications into the distribution centre and caused a small electrical fire in the computer room. Without the sophisticated order entry and shipping system, no orders could be shipped for the subsequent six days. At the peak period of sales for the year, the company could not deliver to its customers. Competitors quickly filled the gap and filled the delayed orders. The one-off significant financial loss in sales was bad, but the long-term effects of departed customers weakened the company sufficiently to make it a takeover candidate in the following year. Within 15 months, the organisation had been sold and merged with a larger competitor.

The consequences of a single point of failure—a modest accident in a car park—caused the dissolution of a multimillion-dollar organisation. A well-designed and exercised business continuity plan would have identified the potential point of failure, defined the impact of such a failure of the computer systems, mitigated the risk, and developed plans to deal with the probability of occurrence. Sales would have been affected somewhat, but critical functions would have continued and major customers would have been satisfied. This example serves to underline that business continuity plans are an obligation to the stakeholders of your organisation: shareholders, employees, customers, suppliers, and regulators. Proactive companies are able to absorb the impact of catastrophic events and continue critical business processes to sustain their business. Unprepared companies suffer significant impacts to sales and market share.

The operations team must ensure that the developed standards and policies are deployed in repeated training and simulation exercises, and that those exercises are reviewed and updated as organisational changes take place. Monitoring personnel must conduct routine audits to ensure that compliance is maintained with both operational plans and logical systems. If the organisation ever moves into disaster status, it is the monitoring personnel that will be key contributors to providing information in the early stages of crisis management.

CONCLUSION

A highly effective digital security programme includes all nine security agenda components along with others specific to the organisation, industry, or evolving threat landscape. Together these will help enable an organisation to mitigate risk, minimise vulnerabilities, and deflect threats; to coordinate appropriate, cost-effective responses to incidents when they occur; and to respond and recover smoothly and efficiently when the immediate attack has concluded. Having such a programme requires that the executive-sponsored, qualified and cross-functional digital security team has opened lines of communication both up- and downstream within the organisation; this team must also receive acceptable levels of input from both business and technical groups. The digital security team must continually build the programme, altering it as needed to maintain strategic internal and external alignments, and reflect new situations. Simulation exercises for attacks and responses must be conducted to determine organisational readiness and indicate areas in need of improvement. The executive management of an organisation with an aligned, enterprise-wide, formalised, and validated digital security programme that is proactive in outlook and continuously updated will attain a high level of confidence that the health of the organisation will be maintained under the most extreme circumstances.

5

The Security Life Cycle

- Organisational Model
- Planning
- Architecture
- Operations
- Monitoring

I n Chapter 4 we described nine common elements of a successful digital security programme. In this chapter we describe ways to implement these successfully in an organisation. We begin by discussing where digital security should reside within the organisational hierarchy to help ensure that it has the authority and influence to achieve its objectives. Next we describe typical phases in the life cycle of a digital security programme and the different activities that should occur in each phase to help ensure each of the nine elements is properly deployed.

ORGANISATIONAL MODEL

While there is common acceptance that much of the implementation and administration of digital security should be the responsibility of the IT group, there is frequently not agreement on who is ultimately responsible for assessing the risks and the security features required to reduce those risks to acceptable levels. Frequently the business looks to IT to address these issues as part of their administration of security, and IT often claims this should be the responsibility of the business. Effective digital security requires expertise from a wide range of functional areas within the business and IT and so it is important that there is involvement of each of those areas.

For example, business process owners should be responsible for determining the appropriate security requirements for information they own, the legal department may be required to set out the regulatory requirements to be met, the IT department is best placed to understand technical system vulnerabilities as well as understanding the options available for providing technical solutions, the human resources department is responsible for determining formalities relating to employees joining and leaving, and so on. If the security agenda is completed without appropriate involvement of all relevant stakeholders, it is likely that the result will be deficient in key areas.

Regardless of where digital security sits in the organisation, it is essential that it has effective links to (and the co-operation of) other relevant functions not under its direct control—for example, public, media, and government relations; physical security; privacy; and business continuity. A Head of Security is central to the success of the digital security programme. In selecting where to place the Head of Security, the CEO often delegates the authority and responsibility to manage digital assets risk in the organisation. In this capacity, the Head of Security must have access to (and receive input from) those at the highest levels of executive management.

In the largest organisations, the Head of Security might report directly to a senior officer in the organisation, as shown in the top half of Figure 5.1. In smaller organisations, it is more common for the Head of Security to report to a manager or director two or three levels below the CEO and, even then, the reporting line usually remains within the IT group. Where the Head of Security is positioned a few levels lower in the management hierarchy, there is a real danger that key security decisions will not receive the level of business support required. In these organisations it is essential that another leader, frequently the

FIGURE 5.1 Digital Security Model

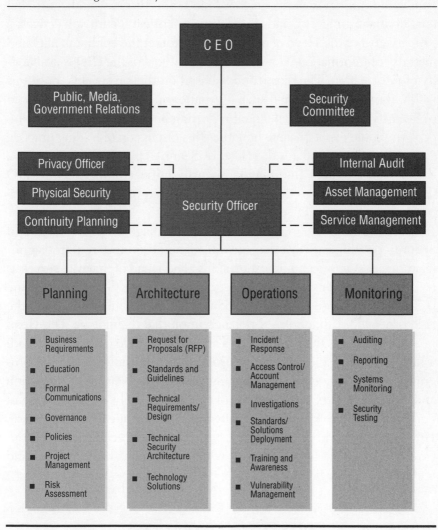

Chief Information Officer (CIO), actively represent and support the wider security agenda at boardroom level (assuming the CIO is in the boardroom). Cross-business executive-level support is one of the key criteria for success of digital security programmes.

Attempting to make strategic decisions that address risks while reporting within the IT group can present additional challenges. For instance, it is possible that the CIO and Head of Security might have conflicting primary security goals. While both officers would agree that confidentiality, integrity, and availability are critical security objectives, a primary goal of the Head of Security is to protect the confidentiality and integrity of information. However, a primary goal of the CIO is availability of information. The distinction is based on their respective positions within the organisation, and such a situation makes a case for the Head of Security having an independent reporting line to senior management.

We should explicitly note here that this discussion of leading practice intentionally differentiates the Head of Security, by whatever title, from the often seen Chief Information Security Officer (CISO). The CISO usually reports through the Head of IT, by whatever title, and has a primary agenda around IT security.

Bearing strategic responsibilities to manage risk, the Head of Security position is clearly executive-level and therefore requires significant business and communication skills. The Head of Security serves as an advisor to other executive managers to facilitate deployment of the technology required to achieve productivity gains while minimising the risk associated with increased reliance upon that technology. The Head of Security directs the organisation's efforts to acquire capabilities to run a highly effective digital security programme and ensure that the programme can provide for the changing requirements of the organisation and its shareholders, employees, and customers. To be effective it is not necessary for the Head of Security to be a technical security guru. However, the Head of Security must have enough technical competencies to be credible with the gurus when confronted with business and apparent technological "absolutes."

PLANNING, ARCHITECTURE, OPERATIONS, AND MONITORING CAPABILITIES

As with most business processes, successful deployment and management of a digital security programme requires a process life cycle that incorporates elements of planning, architecture, operating, and monitoring. This section considers how the security function needs to coordinate its activities with other parts of the business and applies these to the phases of the security life cycle.

As shown in the lower half of Figure 5.1, the model of an effective digital security programme includes the development of four distinct yet integrated elements of a typical process life cycle: planning, architecture, operations, and monitoring (PAOM). Each of these plays a role in ensuring proper execution of the key security agenda items. This framework can assist the digital security architects as they deploy technology to meet the organisation's digital security objectives. Once implemented, the PAOM framework can be used as a model for measuring the success of a digital security programme or segments of it. Agenda items discussed within the context of PAOM are interconnected but can function independently of each other as the organisation moves toward the goal of a fully optimised, digital security programme.

The digital security *planning* team is responsible for tasks such as formalising the organisation's IT governance model, conducting risk assessments, directing security education efforts, managing the formal documentation effort, and providing project management on digital security-related projects. The *architecture* team is responsible for developing security configuration standards, analysing and developing potential digital security technical solutions, and designing the overall architecture for the digital security programme. The *operations* team is responsible for the day-to-day implementation and smooth functionality of systems, applications, and networks. These responsibilities include granting and revoking user privileges, vulnerability and account management, technical security configuration deployment, ensuring security awareness, and responding appropriately to potential issues. The primary focus of the *monitoring* function is to observe and audit systems, examine them for anomalies, and to report on compliance with policies.

The policies, standards, and guidelines agenda items play a vital role in an organisation by granting the digital security team the authority to run the digital security programme and represent the executive-sponsored direction for digital security to the entire enterprise. This direction is presented via formally documented policies that establish

FIGURE 5.2 Aspects of the PAOM Capabilities

Planning	Architecture	Operations	Monitoring
■ Business Requirements ■ Education ■ Formal Communications ■ Governance ■ Policies ■ Project Management ■ Risk Assessment	■ Requests for Proposals (RFP) ■ Standards and Guidelines ■ Technical Requirements/Design ■ Technical Security Architecture ■ Technology Solutions	■ Incident Response ■ Access Control/Account Management ■ Investigations ■ Standards/Solutions Deployment ■ Training and Awareness ■ Vulnerability Management	■ Auditing ■ Reporting ■ Systems Monitoring ■ Security Testing

technical configuration settings for specific technologies according to industry or in-house standards; these policies provide direction for managing digital security throughout the enterprise by implementing guidelines.

The core policy set should:

- Include policies that describe the function of the digital security programme.
- State the importance of, and management support for, digital security.
- Outline a security committee that provides oversight to the programme, establish roles and responsibilities with respect to digital security.
- Identify laws and regulations requiring compliance.
- Outline a framework for digital asset classification, asset management, change management, and waiver management.

Figure 5.2 presents the aspects of the PAOM capabilities. Figure 5.3 links the phases of aspects within the PAOM capabilities with each of the nine digital security agenda items described in Chapter 4.

Planning

The planning capability of a digital security programme is the cornerstone of formalisation of the programme. Capabilities and agenda items should have their roots in planning, whether in the initial creation and deployment of the capability or agenda item, or in their ongoing

FIGURE 5.3 Aspects of the PAOM Capabilities Broken Down by Agenda Item

Agenda Item	Planning	Architecture	Operations	Monitoring
Policies, Standards, & Guidelines	▪ Policies ▪ Formal Communications ▪ Governance	▪ Standards & Guidelines ▪ Technology Solutions	▪ Standards Deployment ▪ Training & Awareness ▪ Vulnerability Management	▪ Auditing
Intrusion & Virus Detection	▪ Policies ▪ Business Requirements ▪ Project Management ▪ Education ▪ Formal Communications	▪ Standards & Guidelines ▪ RFP ▪ Technical Requirements/Design ▪ Technology Solutions	▪ Solutions Deployment ▪ Vulnerability Management ▪ Incident Response	▪ Systems Monitoring ▪ Security Testing ▪ Reporting
Incident Response	▪ Policies ▪ Business Requirements ▪ Project Management ▪ Education ▪ Formal Communications	▪ Standards & Guidelines ▪ RFP ▪ Technology Solutions	▪ Standards/Solutions Deployment ▪ Training & Awareness ▪ Incident Response ▪ Investigations	▪ Reporting ▪ Auditing
Privacy	▪ Policies ▪ Risk Assessment ▪ Governance ▪ Business Requirements ▪ Formal Communications	▪ Standards & Guidelines ▪ Formal Communications ▪ Technical Requirements/Design ▪ Technical Security Architecture ▪ Technology Solutions	▪ Standards/Solutions Deployment ▪ Training & Awareness ▪ Vulnerability Management ▪ Access Control/Account Management ▪ Investigations ▪ Incident Response	▪ Auditing ▪ Systems Monitoring
Physical	▪ Policies ▪ Formal Communications ▪ Risk Assessment ▪ Governance	▪ Standards & Guidelines	▪ Standards Deployment ▪ Investigations ▪ Training & Awareness ▪ Access Control/Account Management	▪ Auditing
Entitlement Management	▪ Policies ▪ Risk Assessment ▪ Education ▪ Project Management ▪ Business Requirements ▪ Formal Communications	▪ Standards & Guidelines ▪ Technical Requirements/Design ▪ Technical Security Architecture ▪ Technology Solutions	▪ Standards/Solutions Deployment ▪ Training & Awareness ▪ Access Control/Account Management	▪ Auditing ▪ Systems Monitoring
Asset & Service Management	▪ Policies ▪ Formal Communications ▪ Risk Assessment ▪ Education ▪ Project Management ▪ Business Requirements	▪ Standards & Guidelines ▪ Technical Requirements/Design ▪ Technical Security Architecture ▪ Technology Solutions	▪ Standards/Solutions Deployment ▪ Training & Awareness ▪ Vulnerability Management ▪ Access Control/Account Management	▪ Auditing ▪ Systems Monitoring
Vulnerability Management	▪ Policies ▪ Formal Communications ▪ Risk Assessment ▪ Education ▪ Project Management ▪ Business Requirements	▪ Standards & Guidelines ▪ Technical Requirements/Design ▪ Technical Security Architecture ▪ Technology Solutions	▪ Standards/Solutions Deployment ▪ Training & Awareness ▪ Vulnerability Management	▪ Auditing ▪ Systems Monitoring
Business Continuity	▪ Risk Assessment ▪ Governance ▪ Education ▪ Project Management ▪ Formal Communications ▪ Business Requirements	▪ Standards & Guidelines ▪ Technical Requirements/Design ▪ Technical Security Architecture ▪ Technology Solutions ▪ RFP	▪ Standards/Solutions Deployment ▪ Training & Awareness	▪ Auditing

maintenance and care. Planning for digital security helps ensure that the programme delivers the level of security that is required by the organisation. Planning accomplishes this in part by ensuring that ad hoc approaches to capabilities and agenda items are minimised or eliminated, that all efforts are driven by business requirements, and that efforts are targeted where the most risk exists.

When these capabilities are in place and operational, the digital security programme begins to take on two characteristics of a highly effective programme: aligned and formal. It has become aligned in the sense that executive management is now directing digital security considerations instead of delegating them. The programme has become formal in the sense that management-approved policies have been documented, communicated as relevant to every member of the organisation, and followed by executing the digital security programme functions. Once a formal digital security programme has been established, the digital security team's focus can shift towards improving and implementing additional security services that involve establishing additional goals, assigning resources, and developing procedures.

Aspects of Planning

Business Requirements   Business requirements establish the need for capabilities, aspects, and items that make up the digital security programme. Each capability and item exists to support one or more business requirements. Requirements function as the measuring stick for capabilities, aspects, and items. If the capabilities and items are meeting the business requirements for risk mitigation, digital security objectives are being met; if not, the organisation must take action to improve the capability, item, or aspect of the digital security programme.

Business Case   A key component of the planning phase is to make a business case that balances desired benefits with the anticipated costs and effort that will be required to achieve those benefits. This is a particularly challenging task because standard return-on-investment (ROI) models are difficult to apply to security. This is mainly because security spend focuses on avoiding loss rather than generating revenues, and the measures for the amount of loss avoided for a given security spend are notoriously difficult to measure with any degree of accuracy. This makes it all the more important to formally clarify at the planning stage what the anticipated costs are of achieving a specific security posture.

Education   The objective of security education is to develop and maintain the skill sets of the enterprise security organisation. Whereas a security awareness programme focuses on IT and end users and topics that address operational systems, an education programme addresses the technical skills of the organisation as needed to ensure that knowledge of leading practices, industry or regulatory issues, and new technologies is maintained.

A frequent reason for failure of awareness programmes is that they are often delegated to IT staff whose capabilities and experience are focused on IT systems, and not necessarily on effective education and communication skills. Given that poor user awareness is a key cause of failure of effective digital security programmes, it is essential that suitably capable individuals are involved in the design and roll-out of awareness programmes.

Policy   This aspect of planning encompasses two fundamental functions: the development and maintenance of security policies that give direction to standards and guidelines, and the development of a waiver framework to manage sanctioned deviations from policies, standards, and guidelines. Performing these functions ensures that the security policies, standards, and guidelines are kept up to date, are enforced, and have approved variances documented in formal waivers.

Formal Communications   This aspect of planning encompasses several fundamental functions not addressed by the digital security policies, specifically the development of procedures for achieving goals and measuring goal attainment within the programme. The process of measuring performance against goals can be reported to the appropriate parties in scorecards. This ensures that progress is sustainable and predictable as the organisation moves towards the goal of having a top-notch digital security programme. This aspect of planning is also responsible for reporting the status of digital security items and capabilities to the CEO, the security committee, management, and employees. Scorecard information is approved by the Head of Security prior to distribution. Digital security information is provided to the planning, architecture, operations, and monitoring teams.

Governance   Governance is the process of management oversight to ensure business risks are identified and remediated; it also ensures that controls are adequately applied throughout the enterprise to reduce risk. This oversight also ensures that management stays informed of current risks and that there is a formal mechanism to communicate both objectives and risks within the digital security programme as the organisation changes. This may take various forms ranging from verbal briefings, to detailed metrics, to formal dashboard-style reporting.

Project Management   Project management within the digital security programme includes the development of the overall programme budget, developing plans for the assessment and implementation of new elements of the security architecture, vendor selection, and contract management for software, systems, and services. Project management is also provided for implementing and improving capabilities and agenda items.

Risk Assessment   This includes defining the scope of analysis, identifying environments and assets for review, evaluating the importance of assets within organisation operations, identifying threats to assets, vulnerabilities, and compensating controls, developing a risk profile for the assessed environment, and developing a risk-reduction plan for the environment.

Systems Development and Maintenance Controls   The operation of secure and reliable IT systems depends on the quality of all elements of the PAOM cycle. Deficiencies in any of these phases typically have adverse knock-on effects on the others. For example, in the rush to implement new Web-facing applications during the dot.com boom, many good practices for managing projects and writing applications were compromised. Good practices for building security into the applications, and for writing secure applications were ignored in favour of functionality and speed to market. This is one of the reasons behind the wide availability and use of applications that are vulnerable to hackers and viruses. These weaknesses can undermine security provided by firewalls and other infrastructural security mechanisms. In these cases, a failure to address fundamental security requirements in the planning and architecture phases has resulted in fundamental weaknesses in the security of the live applications in the operating environment, and created significant challenges to ongoing maintenance.

Retro-fitting security to systems and applications after they have been developed and implemented can cost tens or hundreds of times more than the cost of building security in from the beginning. Also, security that is merely bolted on is frequently a compromise solution with many inherent deficiencies.

Systems development and maintenance controls fall into three main areas:

1. Security and related controls over the systems development and maintenance processes, such as controlling access privileges of programmers to test and production environments. These are described in Chapter 3.
2. Security functionality that needs to be designed and implemented in new or changed systems or applications prior to implementation. The effective operation of digital security depends on the security capabilities of the systems in operation. For many systems and applications that are purchased, the capabilities are designed into the products as options that must be configured for effective operation. However, for systems and applications that are developed in-house or are purpose-built, security features will only be available if they have been included in the specification and build. Frequently the security features of purpose-built applications are missing or deficient in functionality.
3. Systems development and programming practices for designing and building secure applications such as those designed for military purposes. In addition to specific requirements for security functionality, there are numerous precautions that systems developers must take to restrict the vulnerability of those systems to attacks that bypass normal security features. The inherent weaknesses in many Web applications described above fall into this category.

In deploying an effective digital security programme, it is essential that the development environments and processes are recognised as integral parts of the PAOM cycle. Security problems that originate in these areas can be very costly and difficult to correct at a later date.

Architecture

The architecture processes in a digital security programme involve the translation of security policies and objectives into technical requirements, standards, and solution designs. The architecture team establishes a model that defines the integration between technologies, business processes, and policy. One key function in architecture is the development of a formal method or repeatable process of integrating security controls into the design of digital information systems. Architecture functions also include technical research and development of technologies that support the evolution of the system architecture.

Aspects of Architecture

Request for Information/Request for Proposal (RFI/RFP) Development
This entails ensuring that RFIs/RFPs include adequate digital security requirements or documentation, and working with RFI/RFP recipients to clarify details to ensure that digital security is considered as the organisation acquires new technologies.

Technical Requirements Design   An architecture team must be able to describe and map technology elements to fulfil a business requirement.

Technical Security Architecture   This aspect of digital security architecture incorporates the design and structure of the security components that support an organisation's ability to defend its digital frontier. It includes the communication of this technical security architecture to the organisation as a part of the overall security services provided to the organisation.

Technology Solutions   This entails researching and developing new technology solutions for the enterprise, enabling the enterprise to deploy security measures concurrent with the deployment of new applications or infrastructure. The technology solutions function is a formal liaison between the digital security team and the IT group, and provides the enterprise with a mechanism for technical assessment of design alternatives if waivers to policy and standards are required. This aspect is also responsible for assessing waivers that document situations in which a digital asset operates outside of compliance with digital security policy. The assessment of waivers includes identifying options and creating a road map for bringing the digital asset into compliance with policy, or for defining specific instances where it is considered expedient to sanction exceptions.

Budgeting   Careful budgeting is essential for ensuring that individual security plans are implemented to budget and on time, and that funds are available to meet all the requirements in the security plan.

Operations

Digital security operations are those tasks or processes in the security programme that are generally performed on a day-to-day basis to provide security services to the organisation. Because these functions are numerous, they have a strong tendency to be distributed throughout the enterprise. When assessing, designing, or implementing the digital security operations function, the objective is to create the most efficient process that supports appropriate segregation of duties and supports the availability of digital assets. Security operations models can be distributed or consolidated and, in ideal cases, many of these tasks are automated.

Aspects of Operations

Incident Response   This aspect of the operations function is responsible for responding to verified digital security incidents in such a manner as to minimise impact on the organisation. This is accomplished by bringing together cross-functional teams with skills that are pertinent to each individual incident.

Access Control/Account Management   This entails coordinating, creating, and maintaining effective controls for user account management and access controls for all user IDs and access profiles within the enterprise. This may also include the management of third-party access to applications in outsourcing situations and management of business-to-consumer, business-to-business, and business-to-employee operations.

Investigations   The formal analysis of digital assets in support of bona fide digital security incidents is a critical step that precedes the execution of a formal digital forensic investigation. This includes evidence handling and linkages to other pertinent areas, including human resources, legal, and other management functions.

Standards/Solutions Deployment   After a standard or solution has been defined, designed, and tested, it must be deployed into the environment to bring about the targeted returns. Standards/solutions deployment covers the actual implementation of standards or technical solutions into the target environment. Beyond the initial implementation, this also includes deploying periodic updates to existing standards or solutions.

Training and Awareness   This aspect of operations includes developing, maintaining, and deploying the security awareness programme. The security awareness programme should include topics such as password usage, physical security, screen saver usage, virus reporting, "social engineering" behaviours and other topics that ensure the security of the organisation's assets. These may include regular communications regarding the organisation's security status, and other messages that relay not only the importance of digital security but also the awareness that digital security-related events are occurring and being resolved.

Vulnerability Management   This aspect involves tracking exploitable weaknesses and maintaining the integrity of information systems by identifying appropriate safeguards and ensuring that potential points of failure are addressed on an enterprise-wide level. This also includes centralised monitoring and automated methods of ensuring that compliance and configurations are maintained throughout the organisation.

Cost and Benefit Management   To maximise the security for a given spend or to understand whether return on investment (ROI) is being achieved, it is essential to understand both the costs incurred and benefits realised. Both of these are typically difficult to measure, but if no attempt is made it may be difficult to resist budgetary pressures to reduce spending or to determine whether too much cost and effort are being devoted to security.

Monitoring

Monitoring processes in a digital security programme ensure that a management mechanism exists to assess the effectiveness of operational processes and that digital security information required for regulatory or other reports is generated as required. When necessary, the monitoring and compliance function assists with response to incidents and helps conduct investigations, in addition to the formal aspects of monitoring.

Aspects of Monitoring

Auditing   Auditing includes conducting activities to assess the effectiveness of the people, processes, and technology that make up the digital security programme. Assessments are conducted to ensure that policy, procedures, and standards are implemented and followed, testing the real effectiveness of the digital security programme. Auditing identifies scenarios in which policy, standards, and guidelines are deployed and indicates whether the people, processes, and technologies that deploy them are adequate or require improvement.

In addition to determining whether security is operating at the right level for the organisation, it is a responsibility of the audit function to determine whether the organisation is achieving value for money on its security spend, to determine whether the benefits have been appropriately balanced against the costs, and whether the spend on security has realised its anticipated benefits.

Reporting   As required by organisational policy or regulation, the digital security programme provides required management reports to demonstrate the effectiveness of controls and report identified lapses.

Systems Monitoring   A fully deployed digital security programme must be capable of monitoring for unauthorised activity on digital assets, reviewing various log files for unauthorised or unrecognised activity, and tracking the state of health of digital security.

Security Testing   This function is responsible for executing continuous security tests on all digital assets to help ensure digital security counter-measures are working properly.

Designing Security Dashboards

It has become popular recently for organisations to use the concept of "dashboards" or "scorecards" for reporting information that is concise and easy to assimilate, often represented graphically. Many organisations have struggled to implement effective security dashboards because they have focused on the technical information that they have available to report and how they might represent it more concisely, but have given insufficient attention to the requirements of the intended recipient of the information. The following examples illustrate the point:

The Head of Security may require information that indicates significant trends or events that stress the need to take remedial action or make adjustments to ongoing security administrative processes.

IT management and the audit function may be interested in information relating to the performance of security against a number of relevant metrics, such as cost against budget, speed of response to resolve incidents, number of security incidents reported or identified, and so on.

The above two categories typically require significant technical information that can be obtained from system logs and reporting tools. This information is usually readily available and the challenge is in summarising it sufficiently so as not to lose key messages, while keeping the reports manageable.

However, this might not be the case for business and executive management, because they are typically more interested in metrics and indicators directly related to the performance of the business, for example, sales and financial performance. Summaries of technical security statistics are unlikely to meet the needs of these audiences. The challenge is to translate technical security statistics into relevant business terms. Three key considerations that help to achieve this are:

1. Recognition that for security no news is often good news, and that much security dashboard reporting to business management should be by exception.

2. Understanding the thresholds and business measures that are relevant to the intended recipient. For example, a senior executive might not want to be informed of security issues unless they are likely to:

- cause the organisation, or management, to be in significant breach of regulatory requirements.
- result in significant loss of revenues to the business (it is useful to understand what the monetary threshold is to trigger a reportable event).
- adversely impact the reputation or share price of the organisation (again, it is preferable to understand the level of severity required to trigger a reportable event).

3. Consideration of whether the recipient should be expected to take any action as a result of the information reported.

PART THREE

The Approach for Safety

The decision to be part of space exploration has as much to do with possessing drive and ambition as it does with having diverse talents and skills. But such drive and ambition without constant vigilance about safety can come at a high price, even in aspects of space exploration that can now seem routine. Knowing where to look for risks, how to prevent incidents and lessen the impact of crises when they occur, and knowing what it would take to recover from these incidents requires a combination of experience, active curiosity, and healthy skepticism. Space exploration programmes constantly seek to anticipate worst-case scenarios and develop responsive strategies. They work to implement those strategies when needed, adjust them according to the circumstance, and then, just as importantly, move forward when it is deemed safe to do so.

Business organisations at the edge of the digital frontier are often assumed to have what it takes to remain there. After all, they initially had what it took to get there. However, the digital frontier is not a destination;

it is a consequence of the journey toward productivity and profitability. Organisations at its edge cannot indulge in the luxury of settling down and still expect to be secure. The digital frontier moves forward continuously. New hardware, updated software, and faster and simpler means of communication all bring new benefits as well as new risks.

Like explorers traveling through space, business organisations at the edge of the digital frontier must display constant alertness for signs that the situation is changing. There are understood risks that can be calculated, prepared for, deflected, and perhaps eliminated by applying the right approach and utilising the appropriate technology. However, there are still the unknown risks that arrive without warning. The worrying sign of gathering storm clouds is a rare sight on the digital horizon; crises can develop at the speed of light. Although a company might have in place the most up-to-date firewalls and activity-scanning countermeasures, the best authentication, authorisation, and administration processes, and the most informed and well-trained personnel, it still has vulnerabilities that have gone undetected.

This is why establishing a digital security culture within the organisation is a critical step to ensuring the success and ongoing viability of a digital security programme. Being able to quantify risks, prioritise them, and communicate them is important. When the people in an organisation understand the risks faced by the organisation and the solutions that must be applied, the digital security team has less resistance to overcome. A pervasive digital security culture helps create a balance between highly effective security on one hand and high productivity and growth on the other.

Part Three explains why a digital security culture is important and offers recommendations for creating one. It explains why digital security is no longer merely a technical function, but a risk-management operation requiring executive sponsorship and executive involvement. A new approach to risk identification is presented, one that focuses on controlling and containing threats, and mitigating those that are beyond reach. Part Three also offers a new perspective on risk that the traditional return-on-investment approach does not reflect. This new model of the secure organisation is dependent on a fluid strategy built on reality-based scenarios.

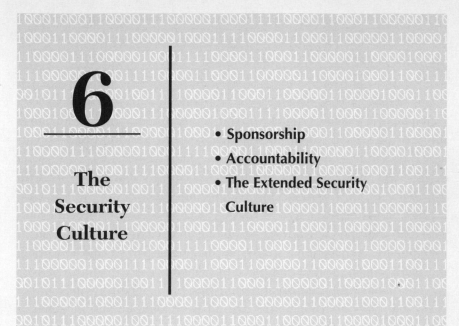

6

The Security Culture

- Sponsorship
- Accountability
- The Extended Security Culture

M any organisations feel confident in declaring that they have a digital security programme. However, for these programmes to be capable of achieving peak effectiveness, they must at least do the following:

1. Deploy all nine elements outlined in the security agenda and do so to the degree that they are fully aligned, enterprise-wide, continuous, proactive, validated, and formal.
2. Be sponsored by the CEO and directed from the executive level.

The chapters in Part Two provided specific information on the first point. This chapter provides details on the second.

SPONSORSHIP

It is vital that the executive who leads the organisation and who charters a mandate for a highly effective digital security programme understands the existing security environment within his or her organisation. Unless the digital security programme in place has attained wide-scale deployment, wholesale changes have to occur to change the *security environment* into a *security culture*. The difference between these concepts is the difference between visiting a city and living there, for example—between spending a few days seeing an ancient city's cathedrals or monuments, and spending a lifetime becoming part of and absorbing the sights, smells, sounds, and pace of that city.

Personnel within an organisation that has a security *environment* know that there are procedures that must be followed and personal or corporate consequences if they are not. Personnel within an organisation that has a security *culture* are aware of and follow the procedures. However, they also understand why those procedures are in place, and they understand not only the personal consequences of a security incident, but the effect a single incident can have on their business unit as well as the entire enterprise.

The first challenge to communicating the necessity for deploying an excellent effective digital security programme may exist in the boardroom or executive suite. A myriad of misconceptions about digital security exists at the highest levels of organisations, including:

- "Digital security is not our problem; it's an IT issue."
- "We have security in place (firewalls, etc.) to protect our networks. Why isn't that sufficient?"
- "Digital security will be a barrier to productivity."
- "We didn't have any problems last year. Why change what isn't broken?"
- "We can't afford it this year."

The rationale behind these misconceptions range from naïve to just plain wrong because:

- Digital security *is* an executive issue, and soon some governments may make it an even more compelling one.
- Network security alone is not enough to keep out a determined hacker or malignant virus.
- A security event of sufficient magnitude will have a much more serious impact on productivity than security countermeasures ever will.
- Past performance is no guarantee of present or future success because threats change and new vulnerabilities appear every day.
- The only alternative to spending on security is spending on recovery.

The Chief Executive as an Agent of Change

Change does not just happen in a large organisation. It requires many hours of planning, execution, and maintenance. To effect change in an organisation's security posture, the CEO and leadership team must become the agents of change and set the digital security programme's goals and priorities.

Instil a Heightened Sense of Awareness

It is imperative that a sense of urgency be established among executives and the board of directors to garner attention and support, and to facilitate co-operation and resource allocation. As the leader of this endeavour, it is incumbent upon the CEO to ensure that this sense of awareness and urgency permeates the organisation and becomes woven into the fabric of the organisation's culture. It must be sustained and nurtured so that it does not dissolve into complacency. This can be accomplished by launching a campaign across the enterprise and acknowledging interim successes on a periodic basis.

Assign Ownership

The CEO and other executives must then assign ownership, monitor the progress at an executive level, and hold those responsible accountable.

This includes, for the most senior executives with relevant roles, outlining expectations in performance contracts, balanced scorecards, and so on, and ensuring reward and recognition is linked to security leadership. It is important that the expectations are not unfair or unreasonable, however. For example, "no bonus unless no viruses" would be too unrealistic an ultimatum. Such measures would only demonstrate a lack of understanding of the complexity of the threats and solutions.

The section that follows outlines some practical considerations and suggestions for accountabilities in the security area.

ACCOUNTABILITY

Build a Digital Security Guidance Council

There must always be one person driving any significant change in an organisation, but that person cannot do it alone. A team—a digital security guidance council—could be assembled to continue the initiative and maintain its momentum. The digital security guidance council must have executive support and must include both executive and technical representation. Ideally, the digital security guidance council should comprise executives who represent the following groups:

- Human resources.
- Legal affairs.
- Business operations areas (for example, manufacturing or engineering).
- Internal audit.
- Finance.
- Information technology.
- Risk management.
- Marketing.
- Facilities management.

The council must also have a defined hierarchy that breaks with tradition and elevates security expertise to a senior level. The council members must have enough influence in the organisation to effectively promote buy-in and instil change at all levels.

The council would also establish strong links with, or in some cases even own the agenda for, key cross-business efforts. Sarbanes-Oxley[1] compliance as it relates to IT controls is an example; these controls extend beyond a security agenda to all business and functional areas associated with financial information.

Establish a Timetable and Monitor Progress

When the digital security guidance council has determined what issues exist and the order in which the security agenda items should be deployed to resolve them, a schedule must be created. Reasonable deadlines should be developed, major milestones should be identified, and programme goals should be clearly established. After the schedule has been crafted, project teams must be assembled and execution begun. It is difficult to create and sustain a high level of enthusiasm for a project that has as its goal the absence of an item or event.

One goal of a digital security programme is to enable an organisation to contain and control a security incident, absorb the impact, and move forward. However, the ultimate goal of a digital security programme is a smoothly running organisation that successfully deflects digital attacks. It is a challenge, therefore, to define short-term successes: How and when does an organisation decide to celebrate the lack of an attack, lawsuit, adverse publicity, injury, and so on? This conundrum, which is somewhat unique to security, serves to underline the importance of identifying the milestones of programme implementation.

A successful deployment of a global vulnerability management programme or an on-time implementation of antivirus software across all desktops should be considered successful milestones, and they should be acknowledged as such. Short-term successes such as these can provide evidence that the investment and efforts are worth it. They can also show to the sceptics and resisters that the programme is working; they may turn neutrals into supporters and reluctant supporters into active participants.

Roll Out an Enterprise-Wide Security Awareness and Training Programme

Security goals should be communicated across the organisation. Effective communication of the goals is essential if the digital security programme is to be a success. The objectives of the communication programme are as follows:

- To educate employees to be able to identify issues.
- To ensure that all employees are aware of their roles and responsibilities on a routine day, as well as during a crisis.
- To ensure that employees understand that the failure to perform a simple but vital security task could result in any number of security events, from unauthorised access to networks to the theft of critical information.

Every person in an organisation, from the mailroom to the boardroom, must embrace and work to the security mindset. Therefore, the security awareness programme must ensure that personnel at all levels:

- Understand the organisation's digital security policies, standards, and guidelines, as well as the employee responsibilities identified within those policies.
- Understand what constitutes a threat to digital assets.
- Be aware of the executive commitment to digital security, which includes seeing executives make the same changes in their behaviour that they request of the rest of the organisation.
- Know who to contact with questions and concerns about digital security issues.

None of this "baked-in" security awareness can come about, however, if the communication is limited to passive means. There must be interactive training and communication. New procedures must be explained and demonstrated to reduce individuals' reluctance to implement security enhancements, and to reduce inevitable levels of frustration that follow any organisational change. For example, the addition of antivirus software that increases the time it takes to boot up a workstation, new logon procedures that require passwords to be changed on a routine basis, and the introduction of biometric devices or random password generators may cause frustration and resistance among employees who are sceptics, or those less comfortable with technology. Proper training and thorough communication can reduce or eliminate such concerns, which, if left unaddressed, could negate the efforts to enhance organisational security.

One fundamental objective of the security awareness and training programme is to change employees' perspectives on digital security by communicating that digital security is important to the health of the organisation. This change in perspective leads to a greater likelihood that employees' behaviour will reflect compliance with policy.

As a means of initiating and continuing these changes, a training and awareness programme could also include such measures as requiring new employees to read the policies of the organisation. They should then sign an acknowledgement that a certain level of understanding of both the policies and the consequences of violating them exists; the annual renewal of such an acknowledgement is wise. It could involve the creation of an automated system that delivers policies to employees, and employs tests that measure employees' understanding of digital security policies. It could continue with coordinated, periodic activities such as those described below that communicate digital security issues to employees.

Common methods to deliver these messages include sponsoring an organisation-wide Security Awareness Week, distributing monthly e-mail newsletters, developing intranet sites, displaying security awareness posters, and holding security-related contests. Such a programme could conclude with the digital security team making themselves available to employees to answer questions or refer questions to those who can answer them. The digital security team should maintain a level of visibility within the organisation while disseminating the vision of the executive-sponsored digital security programme.

Delivering the contents of the awareness programme to employees is not unlike many programme implementations. It should be approached in a formal, consistent method that includes, but is not limited to, the following steps:

- Identify training scope and objectives.
- Identify trainees.
- Identify trainers.
- Secure management buy-in.
- Develop materials.
- Deliver content.
- Measure success.
- Assess, adjust, and repeat.

These steps should assist an organisation in aligning its security culture to the security agenda. The success of the security agenda is dependent on this alignment because it is not just the expert designing the intrusion detection system who is working toward security. Other personnel also make vital contributions: the administrative assistant who remembers to secure his or her workstation by checking for media left in the computer and logging off the system before going to lunch, as well as the executive who adheres to the clear-desk policy before he or she leaves on a business trip.

THE EXTENDED SECURITY CULTURE

In today's world of digital connectivity to customers, suppliers (including IT outsourcers), and even competitors, the desired security culture must be created, cultivated, and tangibly present in the extended enterprise. Those responsible for these relationships and activities must recognise the need to extend the security culture beyond the traditional boundaries and own that responsibility. This has many challenges as customers and others may have less motivation to protect digital assets than employees.

Operating within a security culture implies a heightened awareness of the issues and the risks. In an organisation that has created and now accepts the security culture, every person understands the risks and realises, for instance, that serial nuisances may be more than coincidental occurrences; they may be the start of an attack.

The interplay of people, process, and technology has been identified earlier as one of the security drivers for an organisation. The people variable is the most critical component of any digital security programme. The commitment of an organisation's personnel and its extended community to the principles of security determines the success or failure of the programme.

7

The Risk Frontier

- Modeling and Defining Digital Security Risk
- Approaching Risk Management

Recent world events have dramatically altered the concept of organisational risk. The hazards that organisations face are potentially more dangerous than was previously thought. Threats appear more quickly and can turn into attacks without giving organisations time to prepare effective defences. Earlier chapters discussed the need to be prepared. In this chapter, we examine which agenda items to implement first, and why. Managing vulnerabilities is the responsibility of technical and business experts who have the full support of senior executives. Managing risk is the responsibility of senior executives.

It is the organisation's executive management who must determine objectives, establish the organisation's willingness to accept risk, and ascertain the organisational comfort level about which risks to eliminate, which risks to mitigate, and which risks to accept. It is executive management who must achieve the objectives by investing in the right combination of the nine dimensions of the security agenda and ensuring that the highest appropriate level of security capability is achieved at the lowest reasonable cost.

MODELING AND DEFINING DIGITAL SECURITY RISK

There are a number of frameworks and tools used by organisations to model, identify, and respond to digital security risks. These include the ISF Standard of Good Practice for Information Security,[1] COBIT,[2] ITIL,[3] ISO17799,[4] and the SEI CMM.[5] Each has its strengths and limitations when applied in a particular environment, as each has been developed or evolved for specific constituent stakeholders. Organisations may do well to explore more than one of these options to create a fit-for-purpose response.

Major changes in local or macro threat environments should result in a reevaluation of risks and remedies. This can result in a minor modification or a fundamental change in how an organisation, or indeed a country, models and defines its security risks. Below we use a model, developed in direct response to an event that tragically exposed a macropolitical threat, to demonstrate the application of risk models.

In mid-October of 2001, President George W. Bush created the White House Office of Homeland Security by executive order with the mandate to assess America's readiness to deal with terrorist attacks and to coordinate the detection, deterrence, protection, response and recovery, and incident management of any future attacks. The Director of Homeland Security created a hierarchy for assessing threats to the United States and its citizens and interests.

The far right-hand column in Figure 7.1 lists the threat categories developed by the department: low, guarded, elevated, high, and severe. These threat categories apply as easily to individual organisations managing digital security as they do to the nation. For that reason, they can easily be adapted to describe the digital security risks faced by companies, as shown in the columns to the left and in the middle of the diagram.

A severe threat (category 5) to an organisation is one that would result in a significant risk to a wide customer segment. This is a threat

FIGURE 7.1 Threat Categories

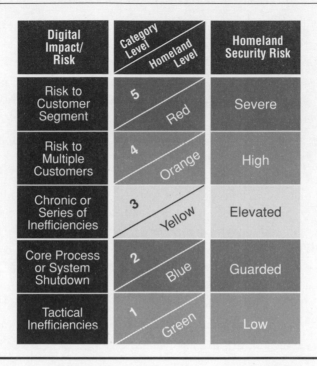

Digital Impact/ Risk	Category Level / Homeland Level	Homeland Security Risk
Risk to Customer Segment	5 / Red	Severe
Risk to Multiple Customers	4 / Orange	High
Chronic or Series of Inefficiencies	3 / Yellow	Elevated
Core Process or System Shutdown	2 / Blue	Guarded
Tactical Inefficiencies	1 / Green	Low

that an organisation will spend significant resources to deflect, and one for which there is no short-term fix. An example of such a threat is the public release of sensitive or private customer information, which would destroy the credibility of the brand image. A high threat (category 4) is one that would present a significant risk to a group of multiple customers. An elevated risk (category 3) represents an event that is the result of chronic or serial inefficiencies, which would impact market share and public and/or employee confidence. An example of a category 3 risk is a Web site that is continually breaking down or coming under attack. A guarded risk (category 2) describes incidents that involve the shutdown of core processes or systems, such as e-mail. Low-risk incidents (category 1) include events that could be described as nuisances or tactical inefficiencies when taken alone.

Homeland Security Advisory System

Low: A low risk of terrorist attack is present. Suggested defensive activities include refining and conducting planned exercises, training personnel, and assessing and mitigating vulnerabilities.

Guarded: There is a general risk of terrorist attack. Suggested activities include ensuring emergency communications systems are in place and functional.

Elevated: A significant risk of terrorist attack exists. Suggested activities include increasing surveillance at critical facilities and assessing threat-specific protocols.

High: A high risk of terrorist attack exists. Suggested protective measures include coordinating security efforts with appropriate authorities and preparing to work under extraordinary conditions, for example, with a dispersed workforce.

Severe: This is the highest state of alert, and suggested security precautions include prepositioning response personnel and redirecting other personnel to address potential needs.

http://www.whitehouse.gov/

Figure 7.2 is the graphic representation of these levels of threat intensity considered in the context of the frequency of occurrence and the level of impact on the organisation. The curved line is the organisation's *risk posture*, which is the level of organisational security as aligned with the threat categories described above. It is the line that signifies the theoretical capabilities of the organisation to mitigate risk (up and to the right of the curve) and the theoretical risk that an organisation is accepting (down and to the left) by choosing to take the chance that those incidents will not occur or will have impacts that are within the limits of tolerance. The shading denotes various levels of incidents that an organisation may experience.

The scale of categories described above is dependent upon both the organisation and the specific situation it is facing. For example, a hack-

FIGURE 7.2   The Security Risk Framework

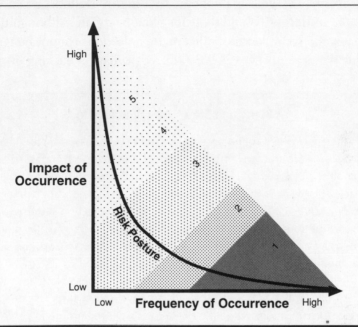

ing event that brings down a Web site is certainly a security incident, although the severity of it depends on the organisation's usage and reliance on that Web site for core business. In addition, a category 1 or 2 threat, combined with other category 1 or 2 incidents within a compressed time frame, could cause the threat level to escalate rapidly. Even a category 1 or 2 threat can become a category 4 or 5 as the result of media attention. Repeated category 1 threats that do not escalate still consume organisational resources that otherwise would and should be used to manage higher level threats.

However, an employee harvesting and selling sensitive or critical information in small increments over a long period of time is also considered a security incident for this discussion, as are the small but incremental attacks of a hacker taking a "low and slow" approach. There is a range of sophistication associated with malicious hackers. The range spans from a "script kiddie" (a hacker with limited technical knowledge and ability) whose goal is publicity, to a highly skilled person whose motives lie in deception and theft for monetary gain. Although the impact that some script kiddies inflict on organisations cannot be ignored, those incidents represent category 1, 2, or perhaps 3 hacking events.

A "Low and Slow" Attack Scenario

When prowling around an organisation's digital assets, script kiddies usually leave destruction in their wake. The category 4 and 5 hacking events are caused by highly-skilled hackers that prowl through and pillage digital assets with a low and slow mentality. "Low and slow" describes hackers who are careful to not trip alarms, trigger detection systems, or let their surreptitious activities be logged. They operate by stealth, gaining access to a system in the same way that military planes fly "low and slow" under the radar to avoid detection by the enemy.

The nature of these attacks makes it likely that these "low and slow" hackers negatively impact organisations on a much larger scale than realised. Organisations without a digital security programme in place are likely to be unable to detect any of their activities most of the time. The activities that are detected will appear to be uncorrelated and, therefore, will be classified as category 1 events; they appear to be little more than nuisances that require little or no attention.

P@tchM4n, an experienced hacker known for his finesse in finding and exploiting system vulnerabilities, conducted an attack on a large financial institution that resulted in a continuous leak of thousands of private customer records over several months. He carried out a quiet scan of the organisation's external-facing network, essentially "casing the joint" as he looked for vulnerabilities.

After finding what he was looking for—a known vulnerability ineffectively patched—he commenced his operations. After gaining administrator access to the server, he skilfully installed a root kit, which is essentially a back door to the system, and tools to assist with further unauthorised access. Using this system as a launch pad, P@tchM4n was able to penetrate the internal network and gain access to servers that supported the customer and financial systems. Up to this point, he had taken extreme pains to avoid tripping security countermeasures, including limiting himself to a few select activities each day or each week. Once the target financial systems were found, they were scanned "low and slow" for vulnerabilities.

He did not find any, but that did not bother him. Nor did it stop him. He set several interim goals and started snooping through files on the system. Fortunately for him, some users, including senior management, had placed their system IDs and passwords into text files, which are unprotected and could be opened by a moderately skillful script kiddie.

Over the next few months, P@tchM4n repeatedly gained access to a database containing customer names, addresses, birth dates, credit card numbers, and social security numbers: a veritable buffet of private information, including detailed data on spending habits. P@tchM4n quietly extracted this information and, without too much trouble, located a buyer willing to pay an exorbitant price for this information.

P@tchM4n's activity was never discovered at the time, and his fun came to an abrupt end after only six months when the network was upgraded. The original system on the network perimeter that he had compromised, and the one on which he had installed the root kit, incurred a hardware failure. The failed system was replaced with another that did not have a root kit on it, did not have the hacker's unauthorised but seemingly legitimate ID, and had been patched for the vulnerability that had been exploited. The ironic result of the system failure was that a hacker's window into the company network was closed.

Incidents like this one create the potential for huge impacts in the area of category 4 and 5 events. Not only was the institution's privacy compromised, but its customers' privacy was compromised even more severely. The fact that the activity had been going on for six months without being noticed, and probably would have continued, is sobering. This trusted system had been severely compromised and the organisation was unaware of the compromise. Although this incident did not become public knowledge, it could have and might still by a variety of means, any one of which could be highly damaging to the financial institution. The customer list could appear somewhere in its entirety with information identifying its origins. It could be recovered as part of a criminal investigation.

Implementing a highly-effective digital security programme would drastically improve not only an organisation's ability to detect this kind of hacker activity, but also increase the chances of preventing this from occurring elsewhere. A vulnerability management programme would help to preclude compromised servers. Strong monitoring capabilities that continuously review server access logs and audit systems for compliance to policies, standards, and guidelines would help identify unauthorised access and identify the presence of IDs and passwords in easily accessed files.

"Low and Slow" Scenario: Lessons to Be Learned

This scenario serves to highlight a critical point that cannot be overemphasised: near-crisis events occur with startling frequency. Many are successfully detected and deflected, and others are effectively contained. This should not, however, be viewed as a triumph. It should be viewed instead as evidence in support of the many dire statistics that indicate increasing rates of successful attack or penetration.

Therefore, the executive management team must determine which threats it faces and what the impact of those threats would be should they occur, disregarding for the moment the actual probability of those threats occurring. Once executives understand the threats, they must also agree on the level of organisational security with which they are comfortable. They must also determine the real level at which the business objectives of productivity and profitability are balanced by security measures, which means understanding that productivity and profitability may be irrevocably compromised if an unlikely or improbable category 5 event occurs but has not been anticipated. The next steps are determining the desired security end-state for the organisation, and then determining the mix of fully-deployed security agenda items that will enable the organisation to reach that state. Using this top-down approach to address threats will probably require significant systemic changes to the organisation, which is why such changes require executive-level involvement and sponsorship.

This approach is controversial because the typical approach to digital security is bottom-up, addressing frequently occurring risks (for instance, category 1 threats) before moving to less probable, higher-impact threats. This approach does not work with high-impact threats if executive management require the digital security team to provide a traditional return-on-investment model to justify the deployment of resources towards mitigating high-impact, low-probability threats. Unable to develop and deliver that model or a message that stresses the strategic nature of managing high-impact risk, the digital security team may fail to persuade management to deploy the appropriate resources. Limiting security investment to those activities demonstrating measurable return on investment to manage risk can leave the management with the mistaken impression that the organisation is doing everything it can.

However, if management does not understand that they have to make some alterations that may not have a justifiable return on investment, the digital security team may be left with the impression that management does not support an enhanced digital security programme since it will not provide the necessary resources. Therefore, the result of taking the traditional, return-on-investment based approach is an organisation in which digital security operates on an IT level and not an enterprise level. The enterprise view of risk contravenes tradition by focusing on developing capabilities to mitigate the impact of a category 4 or 5 threat (rather than focusing on the probability of occurrence) and taking steps to mitigate that impact as quickly as is feasible to maintain clear alignment with business objectives.

The next step in this new model of the enterprise view of risk is the most important: determining what constitutes a category 4 or 5 risk to an organisation. Understanding this enables executives to deploy resources effectively. Specific risks are discussed later in this chapter; however, the foundation of understanding and addressing those risks is determining *the point at which control and containment of the incident become critical to the future of the organisation.* Movement past this point may escalate the situation beyond the control of the digital security team.

It is imperative that executive management and the digital security team know what can drive an organisation to the point at which the ability to control and contain an event is lost. Knowing where that point of control is for an organisation is the key to containing a security event. As has been stated, any event, even a category 1 event, can spiral out of control for any number of reasons. As the damage gains momentum, it will move the event beyond that *fulcrum of control*; virtually nothing can be done to stop the event from materially damaging the marketability, the profitability, or even the viability of the business.

As shown in Figure 7.3, events that are deemed to be above the fulcrum of control are events that executive management must approach from an enterprise perspective. If it has been determined that a certain event, the loss of a mission-critical Web site, for instance, would be a category 5 event, then mitigation strategies cannot be created using a traditional return-on-investment approach. Mitigating that risk must begin immediately, with the understanding that business continuity is the only return on investment.

The goal for incidents above the line is prevention or mitigation of incidents that cause material damage (for example, business continuity issues), whereas the goal for incidents below the line is preventing the escalation of incidents beyond the fulcrum of control (for example,

FIGURE 7.3   The Risk Frontier

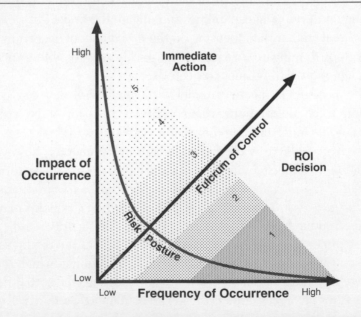

intrusion detection and incident response issues). The prevention and mitigation strategies are accomplished by having in place the appropriate combination of agenda items and mature PAOM capabilities. Implementing the nine agenda items and deploying the PAOM framework creates a systematically safer environment, which effectively moves the organisational risk posture toward the intersection of the axis. This represents the lowest possible impact of occurrence and lowest possible frequency of occurrence. This movement represents an achieved state in which risk is managed to the appropriate tolerance level of the organisation, its shareholders, and employees.

Scenario: A High-Impact Risk Proactively Mitigated

A manufacturing organisation relies on a handful of integrated applications running on hundreds of systems that provide information and services to production fabrication sites across the world. The systems that support these applications physically reside in a single data centre. After recognising the potential impact of a disaster to this data centre, the company conducted a business impact analysis to identify the exact processes that would be affected by such an incident, including the various thresholds of loss associated with extended outages. The analysis revealed that more than five days of outages for these applications would significantly impact the marketability, viability, or profitability of the business. Analysis of the current disaster recovery capabilities of the organisation revealed that it would take 15 days to bring the applications back online and make them available to the fabrication sites.

The executive management realised the organisation was carrying an unacceptable amount of risk should the data centre be destroyed in a disaster. To mitigate this risk, the company decided to focus its attention on two areas: improving its disaster recovery capabilities, and implementing high-availability solutions to reduce the duration of a possible outage. Of the many solutions that could be deemed high-availability, management chose to deploy technology that provided instantaneous replication of all application data to another data centre where "warm," or waiting, systems were on standby in case they were needed. In the event of a disaster at the main data centre, the warm systems could be brought live and the data that had been continuously replicated from the main data centre would be ready and available to employees and customers. Bringing this warm data centre to a live status could be accomplished within 12 hours, leaving the company in a position to maintain marketability, viability, and profitability despite having suffered a major disaster. Essentially, this company addressed a category 4 or 5 incident by deploying resources that would enable it to contain and control the situation should it present itself. Arguably the executive management team's proactive approach turned a category 4 or 5 event into an event that could be classified as a category 2 or 3 event. The organisation's curve, and its risk posture, moved down and to the left in Figure 7.3, and the organization managed its risk.

High-Impact Risk Scenario: Lessons to Be Learned

The impact of similar digital security incidents has different outcomes in various organisations depending on an organisation's ability to control and contain the incident. The ability to control and contain is directly related to the ultimate category that is assigned to the incident. Recall that, by default, executive management must act to immediately mitigate risks for some category 3s, all category 4s, and all category 5s. Further recall that multiple category 1s or 2s that occur within a short amount of time should actually be categorised as category 3s or higher. This reclassification to a higher category level is based on the ability to control and contain a digital security situation. The following scenarios about two much-publicised worms highlight how category escalation can happen and the critical impacts on business due to the inability of a digital security programme to contain and control incidents.

Scenario: An Attack That Was Contained and Controlled

The first worm infected the internal and perimeter network of a large professional services firm, impairing some internal network traffic and crippling the ability to communicate digitally with the outside world. This included its own consultants working at client sites, who were unable to access digital resources on the company's network. The executives at the company brought in some of their own experts to respond to the situation.

Over the next 36 hours, a series of decisions were made with the support of executive management. The decisions led to a near-full recovery of internal network availability and a recovery of the ability to communicate digitally with the outside world. Many difficult but critical decisions were made in the early phases of the response, particularly a decision to shut down all computers that communicate with the outside world. As difficult as this decision was, the company's digital security experts were able to gain executive buy-in that it was necessary to isolate the incident, control and contain the damage, and enable a quick recovery. Within 36 hours, recovery had been accomplished and there was a full resumption of service availability. This rapid and thorough recovery enabled critical time-keeping and accounting services to process consultant hours, leading to invoice generation and payment processing, and avoiding the potential loss of millions of dollars.

This scenario represents a category 1 or 2 event that had the real potential of moving to a 3 or 4, but with an effective, executive-sponsored digital security programme in place the incident was controlled and contained, and did not exceed a category 2.

Scenario: An Attack That Escalated Beyond Containment and Control

A second strain of the same worm infected the internal and perimeter network of a large telecommunications company, impairing internal network traffic, crippling the ability to communicate digitally with the outside world, and effectively bringing customer services to a halt. The personnel at the company were unable to isolate the incident. Furthermore, they were unable to recognise the extent to which the virus had penetrated their environment. Once they did realise the extent of penetration, it was too late to take actions to control and contain the incident.

Having lost the ability to control and contain, the impact of the event intensified over the next 48 hours. This led to lost market share, broken service-level agreements, and lost revenue that severely affected the company's ability to compete and win back customers. Unfortunately, soon after this incident occurred, market conditions took a turn for the worse, making it impossible for the company to redeem its lost market share or recover from lost revenues.

Although the initial event is the same as in the first scenario, the nature of each business changes the intensity of the threat. To a telecommunications organisation, this second scenario represents a category 2 or 3 event. However, because it was neither controlled nor contained, it quickly escalated to the level of a category 4 or 5 event that, when compounded by economic conditions that may not have been foreseeable, eventually led to the company losing a large segment of its business.

Containment and Control Scenarios: Lessons to Be Learned

As these two real-world scenarios point out, although category 4 and 5 events are by definition catastrophic, their impact on an organisation can be lessened. These scenarios emphasise the point that an organisation can only control and contain the situation if it takes a proactive approach and has fortified itself against attack by employing pre-emptive countermeasures such as intrusion detection and incident-response programmes.

If an organisation is not proactive about avoiding attacks, its risk posture remains too far to the right of the axis (see Figure 7.3). Occupying this position means the organisation may not recover from a category 4 or 5 event because no precautions have been taken. Organisations move their curve down and to the left by investing in the nine security agenda items and developing the organisational capabilities detailed in Chapter 4.

Deploying and maintaining a highly effective digital security programme will push the organisation's risk posture toward the intersection of the axes (low impact/low frequency). However, advancing technology will provide a counterbalancing pull away from the intersection and toward the edge of the digital frontier, which is defined in part by continual technological growth. This growth is marked unfortunately by both beneficial and destructive attributes, and the adoption, usage, and reliance on those technologies. If an organisation's prevention and mitigation efforts are not formal, proactive, and continuous—and if they are not aligned to business objectives, deployed enterprise-wide, and validated to rigorous standards—then the organisation's risk posture will move away from the axis by default as advances in technology intensify the risks.

APPROACHING RISK MANAGEMENT

As we have stated, digital security teams focus by default on the lower threat category incidents, and with the nine agenda items in place and fully implemented, this is more easily done. It is up to senior management to identify the most significant threats to the organisation and its business objectives, and deploy resources to manage them, with the focus on prevention.

Defining what constitutes a category 4 or 5 threat to an organisation is an exercise in relativity, and that is why it is a task for executive management. No one else in an organisation has such a good knowledge of the organisation, its risks, and its ability to protect itself from those risks. For example, to an exclusively online entity such as eBay or Amazon, a service outage to an external Web site would be a category 3 or 4, or possibly even a category 5, security incident.

The same incident occurring on a non–revenue-generating Web site for a major oil company, for example, might constitute a category 2 event. However, a service outage to an internal Web site that provides critical supply-chain functionality might rate a category 3 or 4 designation to the oil company, but may not even be applicable to an organisation like eBay. Therefore, the process for determining what the category 3, 4, and 5 events are for an organisation is described as follows:

- High-value digital assets must be identified and ranked.
- Threats to and vulnerabilities within those assets must be determined.
- An impact analysis must be performed.

Armed with the results of this process, executive management should be prepared to set the bar for preventing and mitigating the threats by deploying adequate resources. The executive management team has to take the time to work through potential crisis scenarios. Efficient, adequate deployment of financial, technological, and personnel resources may not, and probably will not, fit the classic return-on-investment scenario that most business enterprises have traditionally used. The decision to deploy resources to address high-level risks cannot be a superficial, bandage-type approach.

Executive management must understand and communicate to peers and board members that appropriate resource allocation is a proactive measure that not only reflects but builds an enterprise-wide organisational commitment. Additionally, such an allocation is justified because of the alignment between business goals and security objectives, and that if it is to fulfill its pre-set goal of establishing top-grade digital security, it must be endorsed at all levels by senior management.

8

Road Map for Success

- **Positioning the Organisation within the Industry**
- **Resource Allocation**
- **Insuring against Digital Security Events**
- **Table-Top Exercises**
- **Executive Radar**

I dentifying threats, putting countermeasures in place to avoid them, and taking steps to lessen the harm they may produce are important procedures to follow before setting out on any journey, and these procedures must be updated en route. Space exploration required years to prepare for each momentous achievement. When setting out to conquer the space frontier, one must prepare for any and every eventuality, as well as for possibilities that cannot be imagined. It takes planning, flexibility, experience, and creativity to withstand a disaster, absorb the impact, and finish the journey.

Life at the digital frontier is much the same. Leading a business organisation to the edge of that frontier takes just as much planning, creativity, strength, and experience as required by the daring explorers of space to meet and overcome known and unknown challenges and still survive. But it is not just about survival. When an organisation has been stricken by disaster, whether malicious hacking has brought down networks and compromised information, or a physical crisis has affected critical infrastructure, an organisation must respond appropriately and initiate its planned recovery procedures immediately—perhaps even before the crisis has reached its conclusion.

To be effective, this set of plans must be understood by everyone in the organisation, not just those at the executive level. The plans must be disseminated and the procedures must be practiced. All the careful planning and detailed documentation in the world cannot prevent the burst of adrenaline that happens the moment a crisis strikes. However, what happens as that adrenaline begins to dissipate is the true measure of how close an organisation is to having an effective security structure in place. When a crisis occurs within an organisation that has instituted and nurtured a security culture, procedures are already under way as the adrenaline rush begins to fade. Emergency response countermeasures are implemented in the midst of chaos, and recovery plans move things forward at a sure, reasoned pace while other organisations have either become suspended in disbelief or are reacting with panic, rushing about in ineffectual circles. In a crisis situation, having a plan and executing it is not just good business sense; it is quickly becoming the fiduciary responsibility of many executive managers.

The idea of digital security, specifically business continuity, is not new. Such plans have been detailed and documented by organisations for years. However, there has never been a time in history when the vulnerability of business operations has been so universally recognised. This vulnerability has been brought onto the executive radar with stark clarity. In the face of global and local threats, the need for digital security procedures assumes a much more prominent role in organisations. Organisations today need a map for successful development and implementation of such procedures, as well as a proven plan for restructuring an organisation to ensure enterprise-wide understanding of the importance of digital security and of fostering a security culture.

POSITIONING THE ORGANISATION
WITHIN THE INDUSTRY

Earlier chapters have detailed the reasons why executive leadership, sponsorship, and direction are critical to the success of a digital security programme. What must be emphasised, however, is that the CEO does not have to understand the technologies as long as he or she understands the risks associated with their implementation and has the ability to effectively balance the organisation's productivity needs and digital security risks.

Because organisations continue to invest in technology for productivity gains and competitive advantage, the edge of the digital frontier is highly dynamic. Organisations at that edge cannot afford to view security as a static end-state. It is not, and it cannot be. The increasing use of and reliance on technology continually pushes the edge of the digital frontier outward, increasing the probability and impact of security incidents. Organisations that want to remain at the edge of the digital frontier must ensure that their risk management strategies include heightened security awareness and fully deployed countermeasures. This inclusive focus on digital security issues exerts an equal and opposite push to lessen the impact and reduces the probability of security incidents while organisations continue to adopt new technologies that enhance their core business.

Pushing back the curve in Figure 8.1 (down and to the left) requires that companies know what their current risk posture is, and what they want it to be. Only then can the decision to move the curve be made. Although moving toward the intersection of the axes for the safety and welfare of the company is the ultimate goal, the first goal must be to move the curve to a position inside the curve of industry peers, as shown in Figure 8.2. Positioning the organisation relative to the competition is important. If a security incident of a critical magnitude occurs and affects an entire industry (for example, if a security breach within one of the major commodity exchanges brings trading to a halt for a period of time), some organisations will absorb the impact and move on. Others that may not have an effective digital security programme in place will falter.

FIGURE 8.1   Forces in Motion at the Digital Frontier

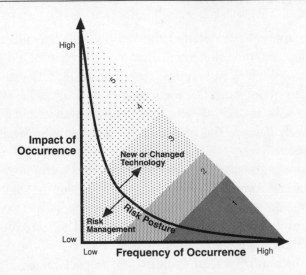

FIGURE 8.2   The Ideal Relative Position for an Organisation

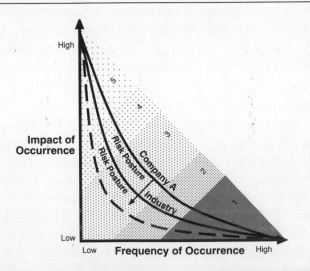

The potential competitive advantage of having a highly effective digital security programme in place cannot be denied. If only a few organisations are able to sustain and absorb an impact that debilitates the rest of their industry, several critical lessons will be learned by the public, as well as by shareholders and employees of those companies and their competitors.

The most important lesson, and the one the market will remember, is that only those few organisations were able to contain and control the damage. Only those few realised that digital security is strategic to the success of the business and took the necessary step of implementing an effective programme. Another important lesson, which the market will also remember, is that the other companies in the industry considered digital security nonessential. This perception by the marketplace can be the competition's greatest exploitable vulnerability in terms of both digital security and market share.

Executives who are thought of as leaders in their organisations and in their industries already have digital security on their radar and are working to push back the risk posture curve to a point beyond industry standards. Every company can effect this change if the CEO is willing to:

- Set the objectives for digital security, ensuring that they align with and support business objectives.
- Allocate resources for a programme to achieve and maintain digital security, including monitoring and measuring the programme itself.
- Promote an enterprise-wide digital security culture.
- Reduce the total risk of security failures while eliminating high-impact events.
- Conceive a charter for the digital security programme that establishes goals and standards for an implementation framework.

When the nine items of the security agenda have been implemented and display all six characteristics of a digital security programme, when the organisation's fulcrum of control has been identified, and when the digital security spending gap that has been allowed to exist has been reduced, an organisation's risk posture curve will begin to move.

RESOURCE ALLOCATION

Every company spends something on digital security. Many executives think they spend enough. The reality is that many, or even most, do not. In fact, when executives are asked, it is clear that most do know what they spend because much of the security spend, if effective, is embedded in the cost of people, processes, and technologies across the entire organisation. In addition, what is spent is often not aligned to the areas of greatest risk or is spent ineffectively, as is the case with other technology-based spend in many organisations.

The biggest problem with determining how much to spend is not only understanding which programmes and countermeasures to implement, but why they are necessary. The answer to this problem is that the correct amount to spend is however much is needed to position the organisation properly on the risk posture curve *and maintain control of that placement*. This enables the organisation to absorb the impact of a significant security event and move forward.

We live in a new world and we face new risks, and resource allocation criteria must acknowledge these facts. Traditional budgeting approaches do not work when the subject is digital security because:

- *The amount of money spent does not guarantee a certain level of security will be achieved.* It is the mix that matters: the organisation, its current security profile, its desired security profile, and the effectiveness of the fully deployed, nine security agenda items.
- *There is not a fixed correlation between investment and return.* The best possible return is invisible: An organisation that runs smoothly and suffers little (if any) damage from a digital security incident.
- *The security purchase is not about image.* It is not branded. In fact, a comprehensive digital security programme is probably something an organisation would not want to publicise, reducing the temptation for hackers to consider it a challenge.

The amount of money an organisation should spend on security is relative to its situation. The only rule is not to spend more than the potential loss due to a security failure. Executive management has to set the parameters of the digital security programme by determining the organisation's strengths and weaknesses (for example, people, process, technology, or infrastructure). Additionally, management must prioritise risks to determine which require immediate action and which can be addressed in a less critical time frame (for example, physical infrastructure, privacy issues, corporate espionage, fiduciary responsibilities, or mitigating future risk by building digital security into plans for expansion). When the parameters have been set, the executive management team can task the digital security team with building the most cost-effective system to those specifications.

Even within the same industry, organisations face different risks. Every organisation has unique needs and capabilities because each has its own competitive position in the marketplace. The decision to allocate resources for digital security cannot rest simply on how much a programme is going to cost, or how much the competition is spending. One of the reasons these issues do not come into play is that each organisation has its own set of core customers and suppliers, each of whom has conditions of their own that have to be considered when the CEO is viewing the enterprise as a whole. An established industry competitor implementing the same agenda item may spend more or less time and money, and require more or less people to run it. However, benchmarking against others in the same industry or companies with other similarities can provide useful input for decision making.

The reasons for the sometimes large differences in implementation and execution costs can vary significantly. Perhaps the first organisation deployed a system that focused on a medium- to high-impact network perimeter because that company's network perimeter contains a handful of servers, applications, and other digital hardware. The second company's network perimeter may contain dozens of servers, applications, and other hardware. The first company may have built expansion capabilities into the system when it was designed, whereas the second company had to take its dense network configuration and retrofit it to include state-of-the-art intrusion-detection capabilities. These and many other variables can and will impact timing and resources in this simple scenario, but the point is that implementing effective intrusion detection in the two companies requires significantly different levels of effort and spending.

INSURING AGAINST DIGITAL SECURITY EVENTS

There are a number of responses to risk: avoiding it, accepting it, and sharing it.

There is a small but growing trend for companies to attempt to insure their way out of digital security risks. There is one serious flaw in this approach: There is no insurance policy that can substitute for having in place a comprehensive, enterprise-wide digital security programme. Why?

Some of the reasons are as follows:

- Buying an insurance policy changes the impact of an event; it does not change the probability of occurrence.
- There is no blanket insurance for security events; no organisation can be insured against everything. Only certain events or occurrences can be covered and, as the business world learned in the autumn of 2001, if you cannot imagine it, you may not be able to protect yourself against it.
- Even when the potential for events can be identified, an organisation must know its probability of risk for that event and the probable extent of damage in order to know how much insurance to buy. If there has been no risk assessment conducted, there is no way of knowing these things.
- Not having identified risk or attempted to mitigate it and not having the ability to investigate an incident would make it significantly more difficult for an organisation to support an insurance claim sufficiently to meet the criteria for insurance settlement.

- If a settlement can be reached, collecting on an insurance claim after a serious security breach will not restore consumer or shareholder confidence. The questions of why and how the event happened in the first place will still be left unanswered.

Although these are valid reasons why insurance cannot replace a security programme, this is not to say that insurance has no place in a comprehensive digital security programme. It is *after* a comprehensive digital security programme is in place that insurance becomes a cost-effective enhancement. The risks have been identified, some have been mitigated, and perhaps some have been made negligible. Proactive countermeasures have been deployed. Personnel have been educated about the risks and ramifications of security incidents. At this point, the executive management team has assessed the organisation's strengths and weaknesses; it knows what assets it wants to insure, and what events it wants to insure against. It may still be a challenge to determine how much insurance the organisation might need or what it might cost to clean up after a disaster. However, those decisions can be reached from a position of strength based on knowledge rather than weakness based on fear.

TABLE-TOP EXERCISES

In 1996, New York Mayor Rudolph Giuliani created the Office of Emergency Management (OEM) by executive order. The OEM reset the standard for coordinated, multi-agency emergency response, and Giuliani's approach brought about an evolution in "what if" role-playing exercises, which he called table-top exercises. Key administrative and technical members of strategic city departments were required to participate in disaster scenarios of many descriptions and magnitudes. Participants were not informed beforehand which scenarios would be conducted in order to make the exercises and the responses as realistic as possible, and so the Mayor could gauge the participants' ability to think on their feet.

Different scenarios focused on how to respond effectively to the immediate situation, whether a natural or man-made disaster, as well as on addressing the myriad of critical issues faced by a city inhabited by millions of people: public safety, sanitation, transportation, and so on. The corresponding needs were prioritised, and the objective of establishing order was aligned with the objective of keeping the rest of New York City's agencies secure and functional. The scenarios and responses were monitored and tested, reassessed and redesigned, then executed again. It was only because of this formal, proactive, administration-wide training and education programme that emergency management personnel were able to respond as quickly and effectively as they did when the unthinkable happened on September 11, 2001.

There is no reason why an organisation cannot apply the same principles and practices to ensure its recovery and continuity after enduring a disaster. Crises of all types—individual and compounded digital events, as well as hybrid digital physical incidents—should be simulated, then reviewed in an ongoing cycle. Table-top exercises and their organisational equivalent serve to heighten awareness of the probability and magnitude of category 4 or 5 events, and to emphasise the importance of knowing what must be done in a crisis, why, and in what sequence. Such exercises are necessary to ensure the full acceptance of a security culture within an organisation and to ensure that disaster recovery and business continuity plans will be effective if they are ever actually deployed. Such exercises are role-playing scenarios on a grand scale that can validate an organisation's plans by assessing the assignment of roles and responsibilities, as well as the actions taken by the executives and senior managers who would be key figures in a disaster situation.

The scenarios are event-driven; the response to a Web site defacement, no matter how severe, is not the same as to a major communications hub for the organisation being penetrated and pilfered, or to a private communications satellite's signal being jammed. The ability of those who are central figures in any scenario to respond appropriately and effectively should be tested. If there is to be any chance of the organisation's absorbing the impact and sustaining the business after an event, insiders have to understand the risks, the ramifications of their actions, and the potential for unforeseen consequences, as well as the various permutations that can mark an incident.

If the risks are unknown, there is no way to plan a response. Panic and chaos are not characteristics associated with successful emergency response procedures, although they frequently seem to be the most widely relied upon. The role of the CEO in the table-top exercises is to identify digital security goals before any plans can be devised or executed. Is the goal functionality within x hours after a category 4 or 5 event? The CEO may have to ignore the boxes on the organisational chart when determining who is best suited to direct the recovery effort for each scenario. These issues are difficult to address, as are the many other questions that must be asked and answered before disaster recovery and business continuity plans can be made. However, they must be asked and answered if the digital security programme that has been painstakingly developed and deployed is to serve its ultimate function: defending the organisation at the digital frontier.

EXECUTIVE RADAR

When a digital security event can impact an organisation's bottom line and maybe even its ability to continue as a business, the CEO must set the security agenda for the organisation. All of the agenda items presented in earlier chapters must come onto his or her radar. When viewed from the perspective of survival rather than return on investment (ROI), digital security is as critical to the organisation as are its products, services, and market share. It is strategically important.

As shown in Figure 8.3, there are several core concerns that have traditionally remained within the scope of executive management: market share, brand image, customer service, growth, and productivity. With the advent of the digital age, another topic came into view: information security. In the 1980s, when few people were using computers, and many companies were only beginning to explore how to use them to enhance performance, security was not an issue other than in the physical sense. The machines and the buildings that housed them had to be protected.

FIGURE 8.3   The CEO's Radar

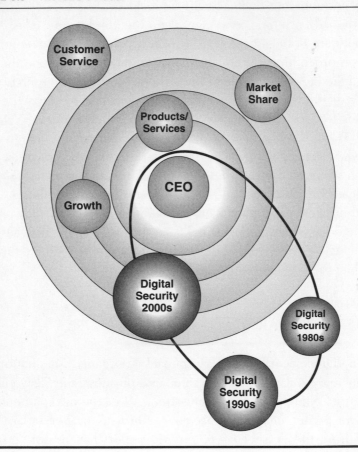

The 1990s brought an explosion of advances in technology and by the end of that decade, even children were online and computer literate. But in the fervour of growth and productivity increases, security was still largely overlooked despite the development of a disturbing and growing trend of malicious, computer-related events directed at large corporations. The impact of global terrorism has finally brought the entire concept of digital security onto the radar of executive concerns.

Now, digital security affects nearly every aspect of an organisation's life and culture. When critical systems go down, whether physically or logically, everything relying on them or connected to them stops. If private or sensitive information is released on the Internet, it can be copied and stored by millions of users; it may be in cyberspace forever. If an incident affects a large segment of the public and the media focus their attention on it, the corporate image may suffer.

It is up to the CEO to ensure that a digital security culture not only pervades the organisation, but exerts an influence on every aspect of it. Security awareness must be the gravitational force that keeps everything else—market share, brand, customer service, productivity, and growth—in perpetual motion at the edge of the digital frontier.

APPENDIX A

Security-Related Laws and Regulations

A t a number of points in this book, reference is made to the importance of applicable laws and regulations in determining an organisation's security requirements. Failure to understand and comply with these can have severe personal and corporate consequences. This poses a number of significant challenges, for example:

- A number of laws and regulations are new and their interpretations are not well understood.
- In some instances older laws are interpreted in the context of the digital world.
- Most organisations are subject to the laws and regulations of a number of countries; these laws and regulations can be very complex or even present conflicts.
- Compliance with some legislation is extremely hard to achieve and enforce.

Ascertaining and interpreting all the applicable laws and regulations is not a job for the "gifted amateur." It is important to entrust this to suitably qualified professionals.

In this appendix we provide a brief overview of some of the key issues facing organisations in this area and a variety of illustrative country-specific references for further information.

BALANCING COMPETING INTERESTS

The world's security-related laws and regulations have to strike a delicate balance between three main interests:

- The interest of commerce and private individuals in data security, in particular in maintaining the security of computer systems and ensuring secure communications.
- The need to detect and investigate crime and to maintain national security.
- The preservation of fundamental rights (human rights in the widest sense) such as privacy, free speech, and property rights (both tangible and intangible).

Deciding where the appropriate balance lies requires a consideration of national priorities, and consequently each country strikes this balance at a different point. China, for example, extends the concept of national security to include the preservation of the state as currently constituted, and for this reason ranks it much higher than freedom of speech by imposing stringent controls on access to and the dissemination of information online. In other countries, most notably the United States, the investigation and detection of crime with a particular emphasis on terrorism has, for obvious reasons, become a much higher priority in recent years. This is reflected in recent legislation such as the USA PATRIOT Act of 2001 and the Homeland Security Act of 2002.

This Appendix concentrates on laws from jurisdictions that have a substantial impact globally. Thus, both U.S. and EU laws are very important because they exert a strong gravitational pull on other countries' legal systems; if a country wishes to help its local businesses to trade with either, it helps if your laws and regulations are compatible. International organisations, such as the Organisation for Economic Co-operation and Development (OECD) and the United Nations Commission on International Trade Law (UNCITRAL), develop recommendations and models that guide the global development of security-related laws and regulations. These, too, are discussed here. Most national laws contain similar provisions; where those provisions are radically different from those of other countries, it is likely that they will be forced to change because of the pressure to conform with existing global models.

Cross-Border Issues

In today's interconnected world it is common for both commercial and private information transactions to have a cross-border component. A nation's laws apply to activities carried out within that nation's territory, so a transaction with a cross-border element is likely to be subject to more than one set of security-related laws and regulations. To complicate matters further, the online actions of residents may be subject to their home laws and regulations, extended to those elements of the transaction that take place elsewhere. The result may be that two or more sets of national laws and regulations apply to a particular element of an online activity.

Sources of Security-Related Laws and Regulations

A later section in this Appendix, Examples of National Security-Related Laws and Regulations, gives some examples of national laws and regulations. However, it must be recognised that none of these is a complete national code covering information security. There are three reasons why this is so:

1. The meaning of a law or regulation is, ultimately, the meaning given to it by judges in court. It is only possible to understand a

law or regulation fully by examining how judges have applied it to particular cases, and even then it must be recognised that the courts develop their understanding over a period of time. Interpretations and application of the law, therefore, can change.

2. Specific laws and regulations only have meaning in the wider context of that country's entire body of law. To take a well-known example, the U.S. Constitution plays an important part in deciding the legal effect of a particular act or regulation, and in determining whether it is in fact a valid law. Even in countries with no formal constitution, such as the United Kingdom, judges interpret the law in the light of other laws. In the context of information security, the UK Human Rights Act 1998 requires judges to interpret security legislation so as to be compatible with the fundamental rights protected by the Act.

3. Finally, aspects of information security are dealt with by extending existing laws to cover new facts. For example, in some countries the preservation of property rights in information systems is achieved by extending the law of trespass to land or goods. The scope of these extensions, and what they mean in an information security context, can only be determined by reading the decisions of the courts.

What this means is that for any given country there is no clear and complete statement of its information security laws and regulations. Even if such a code were produced, understanding its application to a particular set of facts would still require specialised legal advice.

DATA SECURITY

The maintenance of the security and integrity of computer systems has been recognised as a matter of fundamental importance for over 20 years. So serious is this matter that most countries have created criminal offences that specifically address the main risks to security. The OECD published a report in 1986 setting out the fundamental principles that such laws should cover, the most important of which are:

- Unauthorised access such as hacking.
- Interference with the contents of computer systems.
- Fraud, where the deception is of a computer rather than a person.

One international instrument in this area is the Council of Europe Convention on Cybercrime of 2001, which in addition to the matters above covers illegal interception and content-related offences such as child pornography.

The majority of the world's countries have introduced legislation creating computer system-specific crimes, and examples for several countries are given later in this Appendix (Examples of National Security-Related laws and Regulations), Part 6.

These laws tend to criminalise interferences with particular computer systems, but not communications between those systems. Secure communication between computer systems is a matter of fundamental commercial importance.

For matters such as inter-bank financial communications, it is also critical for the continued stability of society as a whole. Security of communications has two main aspects:

1. *Confidentiality of communication.* This is achieved through technological solutions using, for example, encryption technology. Most general application laws and regulations on this matter deal with the interface between encryption technology and crime and national security investigation (see Detection and Investigation of Crime and National Security Matters later in this Appendix). However, in those sectors of activity that are regulated for stability and soundness (the financial services sector in particular), it is common to find laws or regulations that mandate the use of encryption technology and other security controls to preserve the confidentiality of records and communications.

2. *Authentication of communications.* Where a communication is to have legal effect—for example, creating rights and obligations between the communicating parties—there is an interest in being able to authenticate the sender of the communication and its contents. Electronic signature technology is widely adopted,

or at least recommended, for this purpose. However, the general body of most countries' laws predates the introduction of computing and communications technology, and often makes extensive reference to signatures. The age of this legislation and the way it has been applied by the courts often suggest that only handwritten signatures can satisfy the law's requirements.

For this reason, many countries have introduced laws that grant the same legal effectiveness to electronic signatures as to handwritten signatures. These laws fall into two main categories:

1. Those such as the EU Electronic Signatures Directive 2000, which confers the greatest legal effectiveness on electronic signatures that are created in conjunction with identity certification by third parties (essentially ANSI X.509 signatures).
2. Those that treat electronic signatures as equivalent to handwritten, irrespective of the technology used, so long as the electronic signature provides sufficient evidence of the identity of the signatory, the intent to sign, and the integrity of content (for example, the U.S. Electronic Signatures in Global and National Commerce Act 2000 (E-Sign) and the UNCITRAL Model Law on Electronic Signatures 2001).

DETECTION AND INVESTIGATION OF CRIME AND NATIONAL SECURITY MATTERS

There is a clear conflict between the interest in maintaining data security examined earlier, the need for effective detection and investigation of crime, and the maintenance of national security. This need has become more urgent following the recent increase in international terrorist activity.

Some national security organisations—for example, the National Security Agency (NSA) in the United States and the Government communications Headquarters (GCHQ) in the United Kingdom—are reputed to have sufficient computing resources to maintain a reasonable level of surveillance over encrypted communications. However, law enforcement agencies and other bodies connected with national security lack these resources.

Initially, a number of governments proposed to deal with this issue by requiring all encryption keys to be escrowed with a government agency; in this way, encrypted communications could be examined when needed. These proposals were hotly contested on two main grounds: first, that any disclosure of encryption keys immediately compromised the discloser's security; and second, that the track record of government agencies suggested that they could not be trusted to be competent in preserving the absolute security of those keys. There was also a clear conflict between the rights of privacy and freedom of speech. By the second half of the 1990s these proposals had been abandoned.

The most common way in which this conflict of interests has been resolved is by conferring on law enforcement and national security bodies the right to demand copies of computer-stored or transmitted information in specified circumstances. Where that information is encrypted, the holder of the encryption key has the obligation to provide the information in unencrypted form. This approach allows appropriate safeguards to be built into the system for demanding information so as to protect the other interests involved: The preservation of data security, the protection of privacy and confidentiality, and the right to free speech. This is normally done by requiring the body that seeks the information to obtain a warrant and incorporating judicial oversight and appeal procedures into the process.

To ensure that the ability to track communications remains available for sufficient time to enable law enforcement agencies to act, it is also common to require Internet Service Providers (ISPs) and other communications intermediaries to retain traffic and other data for specified periods of time. This type of obligation has been controversial, in large part because of the cost of data retention and of making it available. In the United Kingdom, for example, data retention legislation is currently in place; at the time of writing, however, the UK government is consulting on how best to modify this legislation for the long term.

A further level of control over encryption technology was introduced by export control laws, whose primary aim was to prevent encryption technology from being exported to "rogue" states. These laws have recently been relaxed because of the commercial need to use encryption to protect on-line communications, though some restrictions are still in place. Laws that attempt to prevent the use of encryption inevitably come into conflict with laws that protect freedom of speech, as many countries interpret freedom of speech as meaningless if that speech cannot also be private—surveillance constrains what a person is willing to say. An amusing example of this conflict arose over Zimmerman's PgP software, which the U.S. government argued could not be exported. However, it was not possible to prevent advocates of encryption for privacy from passing through U.S. airports wearing T-shirts on which the encryption algorithms were printed because those T-shirts were protected expression under the U.S. Constitution!

The need to monitor some communications for reason of crime detection or national security is in clear conflict with the right to privacy, as well as the need for commercial confidentiality. For this reason, interception of communications without lawful excuse is normally made a criminal offence. This provides some deterrent to private espionage activities. State interception of communications is usually made subject to prior authorisation by an appropriate supervisory body; the need for secrecy means that this is normally not a court, but instead an administrative body. Applications for authorisation need to be justified on grounds specified by law, which include matters such as the interests of national security, the prevention or detection of serious crime, and safeguarding the economic well-being of the state.

The extent to which the administrative body that controls interception and surveillance publishes information about interception activities depends on the state's attitude towards freedom of information. In the United States, the president's Foreign Intelligence Advisory Board makes frequent public statements. The UK's Interception of Communications Commissioner submits an annual report to the prime minister that is subsequently laid before Parliament and published.

FUNDAMENTAL RIGHTS

Security-related laws and regulations often impact the fundamental rights of citizens. Laws on data security and laws on crime and national security, as we have seen in the previous two sections, need to strike a balance between the interests they are trying to protect and the preservation of these fundamental rights.

Additionally, it is important to note that the laws protecting these fundamental rights often have security implications. For example, in cross-border data processing contracts it is necessary to comply with the privacy laws at both ends of the transaction, and possibly those of any intermediary countries—countries that may impose data security obligations on the holders of personal information.

Privacy

The fundamental right that is most obviously linked to security is that of privacy. Because electronic record keeping and communications are thought to pose greater risks to privacy than print publication or the spoken word, many countries have instituted special legal and regulatory regimes to protect data privacy (normally described as data protection regulation). Usually only personal privacy is protected, as opposed to the privacy of corporate information; however, some states (Switzerland, for example) protect corporations equally with private persons. One of the earliest data protection laws was that of the German Lande of Hesse in 1970, and the primary international instrument of modern data protection laws is the OECD Guidelines on the Protection of Privacy and Transborder Flows of Personal Data 1980.

Data privacy laws fall into two main types:

1. Laws that enforce data privacy through a national regulator such as the UK's Information Commissioner. These tend to be derived from, or devised to coordinate with, the EU Directive on Data Protection 1995. Holders of personal data need to register

the fact that they are holders of personal data, and complaints can be made to the regulator who can take enforcement action.

2. Laws which grant private rights of data privacy which are enforced through the courts through litigation. U.S. state privacy laws tend to adopt this model.

There is a reasonable degree of consensus worldwide on the nature of data privacy rights: obtaining and disclosing data should be undertaken fairly, and proper security precautions should be taken to preserve data privacy. Some countries, particularly those adopting the EU model, also give the right for personal data not to be used unfairly by its holder.

Free Speech

Security laws also affect free speech, as we have seen in the section entitled Detection and Investigation of Crime and National Security Matters. Conversely, free speech laws also affect security by limiting the state's power to prevent communications of which it disapproves. National law approaches to the protection of free speech depend on whether it is seen as an absolute right or as a right to be balanced against other rights and interests.

Most European states have adopted the European Convention on Human Rights, which specifically states that the protection of free speech is a balancing exercise. European security laws therefore tend to set out procedures that are designed to strike the appropriate balance, such as the safeguards built into laws relating to the interception and surveillance of communications (see Detection and Investigation of Crime and National Security Matters in this Appendix).

Other states, most notably the United States, see free speech as an absolute, and the First Amendment to the U.S. Constitution specifically states that Congress "shall make no law...abridging the freedom of speech." This strong prohibition on encryption export controls has been used to strike down a number of Internet-related laws as unconstitutional. For example, the U.S. Child Online Protection Act 1998, which makes it a crime for anyone to make available for commercial purposes on the Web material that is "harmful to minors" unless that person has restricted access by minors by requiring a credit card number, was first declared unconstitutional in 1999. The question is now before the Supreme Court for resolution.

Property Rights

For centuries the law has protected rights to property. These rights can be of real use in preserving computer security against intrusions such as spam e-mails, hacking, denial-of-service attacks, and screen-scraping activities. All of these have at some time been considered trespasses or infringements upon the system owner's property and related rights in various jurisdictions. Many of these activities are also criminal offences, but in general only the state can act to enforce criminal laws and often has insufficient resources and expertise to do so. By using the laws that protect property rights, the owner of a computer system may be able to take immediate action against this type of wrongdoing and retain control of the legal processes involved.

We do not focus here on the analysis of this complex and diverse area of law. However, it is unlikely that a court will find an invasion of property rights unless the activities of the person in question are so extensive as to substantially impair the operation of the computer system. Thus a few spam messages will probably give no right of action, but a volume of spam that slows down or overwhelms servers may well be considered as an infringement upon property rights. Where an infringement of property rights is found, the system owner is normally able to obtain an injunction to prevent further invasions. This is an extremely effective remedy because failure to comply is a contempt of court and may result in imprisonment.

The problem of spam, both for recipients and because of the diversion of computing resources it creates, for ISPs and recipient organisations, is increasingly being addressed by antispam laws. These either give private rights of action against the spammer or create new criminal offences (for example, the EU Electronic Communications Privacy Directive 2002).

CONCLUSIONS

Security-related laws and regulations are extremely diverse, reflecting widely different national priorities and traditions. This diversity, however, is found more in the enforcement and control mechanisms through which individual countries ensure compliance with their laws, rather than in the underlying principles that those laws seek to implement. There is a surprising degree of international consensus about how best the law should protect and maintain the security of computer systems and electronic communications.

This does not, unfortunately, mean that system security complies with every country's laws if it follows the principles set out in this short Appendix. As always the devil is in the detail, and close analysis of the relevant national laws and regulations is always necessary to ensure lawful and effective security. Global organisations, or even those organisations that trade across borders, apply their headquarters' national laws on an entity-wide basis at their peril.

EXAMPLES OF NATIONAL SECURITY-RELATED LAWS AND REGULATIONS

Following are selected examples of national security-related laws and regulations. These are chosen as salient examples of the different ways in which the matters discussed in this Appendix are treated, but by no means comprise a complete list for any of the countries mentioned.

Australia

Commonwealth Cybercrime Act 2001. For additional information, see http://www.austlii.edu.au/au/legis/cth/consol_act/ca2001112/NSW.

Crimes Act 1900. This act was altered by virtue of the Crimes Amendment (Computer Offences) Act. For additional information, see http://www.austlii.edu.au/au/legis/nsw/consol_act/ca190082/.

Crimes (property damage and computer offences) Act 2003, Section 5. This Act updated the Crimes Act 1958. For additional information, see http://www.austlii.edu.au/au/legis/vic/consol_act/cdacoa2003416/s5.html.

Canada

National Defence Act 2001, Part V.1 Communications Security Establishment. For additional information, see http://laws.justice.gc.ca/en/n-5/84610.html.

Security of Information Act 2001—enacted 1985, updated 2001. For additional information, see http://laws.justice.gc.ca/en/O-5/index.html.

Personal Information Protection and Electronic Documents Act 2000. This Act is being implemented in three stages from 2001 to 2004. For additional information, see http://www.privcom.gc.ca.legislation/02_06_07_e.asp.

The Bank Act 2003. For additional information,
see http://laws.justice.gc.ca/en/b-1.01/sor-2003-61/18990.html.

Insurance Companies Act 2003. For additional information, see http://laws.justice.gc.ca/en/I-11.8/sor-2003-63/142898.html.

Co-operative Credit Associations Act 2003. For additional information, see http://laws.justice.gc.ca/en/c-41.01/sor-2003-64/77573.html.

Trust and Loan Companies Act 2003. For additional information, see http://laws.justice.gc.ca/en/t-19.8/sor-2003-69/183889.html.

Privacy of Personal Information Act 2002. Intended to be enacted by 1 January 2004. Not yet law. Act respecting access to documents held by public bodies and the protection of personal information. Latest update is 2002. For additional information, see http://publicationsduquebec.gouv.qc.ca/dynamicsearch/telecharge.php?type=2&file=/A_2_1/A2_1_A.html.

Denmark

Act on Processing of Personal Data, Act No. 429 of 31 May 2000, entered into force on 1 July 2000. The act implements EC Directive 95/46/EC on the protection of individuals with regard to the processing of personal data and on the free movement of such data. For additional information, see http://www.datatilsynet.dk/eng/index.html.

Act on Electronic Signatures, Act No. 417 of 31 May 2000. The act implements EC Directive 1999/93/EF of 13 December 1999 on Digital Signatures and their use, classes of Certificates, Certificate Authorities and their Audit, etc. For additional information, see http://www.videnskabsministeriet.dk/cgi-bin/doc-show.cgi?doc_id=41719&leftmenu= LOVSTOF, or http://www.digitalsignatur.dk/.

Rules on electronic invoicing, Act on VAT of 8 August 2003 and related Ministerial Order of 12 December 2003. The act and Ministerial Order implement the EC Directive 2001/115/EC on VAT invoicing, notably electronic invoicing (Requiring Electronic Signatures or secure EDI).

Act on Marketing, Act No. 699 of 17. July 2000 with later amendments. Enforces warranties related to electronic trade and sets limitations to the use of e-mails in Marketing (Opt in), etc. Implements several EC Directives and internal Danish rules.

Act on Bookkeeping Act No. 1006 of 23 December 1998. Implements the rules on accounting systems, accounting data and other accounting materials, including the protection of such materials. For additional information, see http://www.eogs.dk/.

Common Act on Crime, Act No. 814 of 30/09/2003. Contains various paragraphs against hacking, theft, and misuse of data. For additional information, see http://www.retsinfo.dk (All Danish Laws).

European Union

EU Directive 95/46/EC on the Protection of Individuals with Regard to the Processing of Personal Data and on the Free Movement of Such Data. For additional information, see http://www.dataprivacy.ie/6aii.htm.

India

Information Technology Act 2000. For additional information, see www.mit.gov.in/it-bill.asp.

Information Technology (Certifying Authority) Regulations, 2001. For additional information, see www.mit.gov.in/rules/main.asp.

Communications Convergence Bill 2000. This bill is still at draft stage. For additional information, see www.mit.gov.in/conbill.pdf.

Malaysia

Computer Crimes Act 1997. The Government is in the process of drafting a new piece of legislation on Personal Data Protection. For additional information, see http://www.ktkm.gov.my.default.asp.

Netherlands

Privacy Act 2000.

Computer Criminality Act 1998.

Poland

Protection of Classified Information Act 1999.

Electronic Signature Act 2001.

Act on Provision of Services by Electronic Means, 2002.

Unfair Competition Act 1993.

Database Protection Act 2001.

Polish Accounting Act 1994.

Singapore

Computer Misuse Act 1993. Amendments: Computer Misuse (Amendment) Act 1998; Computer Misuse (Amendment) Act 2003. For additional information, see http://agcvldb4.agc.gov.sg/legislation/htdocs/bills.html.

South Africa

Electronic Communications and Transactions Act 2002.

United Kingdom

Data Security

Electronic Communications Act 2000. This law, together with the Electronic Signatures Regulations, implements the EU Electronic Signatures Directive and sets out a statutory regime for determining the legal validity of electronic signatures.

Electronic Signatures Regulations 2002 SI 2002/318.

Computer Misuse Act 1990. This law introduces three criminal offences relating to computer security:

1. Unauthorised access to a computer system;
2. Unauthorised access with intent to commit a further serious criminal offence; and
3. Unauthorised modification of the contents of a computer system.

Detection and Investigation of Crime and National Security Matters

Regulation of Investigatory Powers Act 2000. This law codifies the powers of law enforcement bodies and the security services to intercept communications, conduct surveillance activities, and secure evidence.

Anti-Terrorism Crime and Security Act 2001. This law makes various provisions to assist the prevention and detection of terrorist crimes. The most important, in the context of this Appendix, is the power to require ISPs and telecommunications operators to retain various categories of communications data to which access may be necessary for the purposes of fighting terrorism. Detailed provisions about the data that must be retained are set out in the Retention of Communications Data (Code of Practice) Order.

Fundamental Rights

Data Protection Act 1998. This law implements the EU Data Protection Directive, imposing obligations on collectors, holders, and users of personal data and controlling the export of that data to countries that do not provide adequate data protection.

Privacy and Electronic Communications (EC Directive) Regulations 2003 SI 2003/2426.

These regulations make unsolicited commercial emails to private individuals a criminal offence unless the recipient has opted in to a scheme giving notice that they are willing to receive such emails. The regulations also cover automated telephone calling systems and unsolicited commercial faxes.

Human Rights Act 1998. This law implements the European Convention on Human Rights. It obliges the courts to interpret other laws, so far as possible, to be consistent with the rights set out in the Act. Where this is not possible the court can make a declaration that the law is incompatible with the Human Rights Act.

United States

Current Legislation

August 13, 2003, U.S. Federal Financial Proposed Interagency Guidance on Response Programmes for Unauthorized Access to Customer Information and Customer Notice (includes an obligation to notify customers of security breaches). This proposed Guidance interprets section 501(b) of the Gramm-Leach-Bliley Act and the provisions of the Security Guidelines. It describes the Agencies' expectations that every financial institution develop an incident response programme to protect against and address reasonably foreseeable risks associated with internal and external threats to the security of customer information maintained by the financial institution or its service provider. The proposed Guidance further describes the components of a response programme, which includes procedures for notifying customers about incidents of unauthorised access to customer information that could result in substantial harm or inconvenience to the customer.

Potential Legislation

H.R. 3159 Government Network Security Act of 2003. Under review by the full Senate. This Act requires require Federal agencies to develop and implement plans to protect the security and privacy of government computer systems from the risks posed by peer-to-peer file sharing.

H.R. 2517 Piracy Deterrence and Education Act of 2003. Under review by Senate subcommittee. The Piracy Deterrence and Education Act directs the Federal Bureau of Investigation (FBI) to develop a programme deterring members of the public from committing acts of copyright infringement by offering on the Internet copies of copyrighted works, or making copies of copyrighted works from the Internet, without the authorisation of the copyright owners.

H.R. 2214 Reduction of SPAM Bill. Under review by a House of Representatives subcommittee. The Reduction of SPAM Bill will allow consumers to opt out of any commercial e-mail they choose not to receive and require spammers to adhere to this opt-out policy. Those who falsify their e-mail identity will be subject to criminal penalties.

Corporate Information Security Accountability Act of 2003 (proposed October 21, 2003). Intended to protect public safety, the economy, and shareholder investments by requiring public companies—as part of their annual report under the Sarbanes-Oxley Act—to include a certification by an independent party that they conducted an assessment of their computer information security in accordance with standards prescribed by the Securities and Exchange Commission.

Sarbanes-Oxley Act. Passed in 2002, this act places strict requirements on company boards and officers to proactively prevent mishandling of information.

Gramm-Leach-Bliley Financial Services Modernization Act. This act mandates strong protection of personal financial information.

California SB 1386 (the California Data Security Act). This act requires control of privacy of an individual's financial information.

New York Reg. 173. This regulation mandates the active encryption of sensitive financial information sent over the Internet.

Homeland Security Information Sharing Act (HSISA, H.R. 4598), Security Rules and Regulations. This Act promotes the sharing of critical homeland security threat information between federal intelligence agencies (including the FBI) and "state and local personnel" (governors, mayors, other elected officials, first responders, and certain private entities) while continuing to protect sensitive sources and collection methods information.

Healthcare Insurance Portability and Accessibility Act (HIPAA). This act places liability on anyone who fails to properly protect patient health information, including bills and health-related financial information.

Homeland Security Act of 2002, H.R. 5005 (November 25, 2002). Congress has approved the Homeland Security Bill, which creates a new Cabinet-level post to oversee and coordinate U.S. domestic security interests against terrorism. The Bill has provisions that deal with cyber-terrorism and powers for obtaining information from computer and ISP sources. One important change allows ISPs to be protected against suits from customers for revealing private information to law enforcement agencies.

U.S.A. PATRIOT Act (Public Law 107-56). Uniting and Strengthening America by Providing Appropriate Tools Required to Intercept and Obstruct Terrorism. The Congressional response to the terrorist attacks of September 11, 2001, (October 26, 2001).

Federal Information Security Management Act of 2002 (FISMA). This act requires the Chief Information Officer (CIO) of each federal agency to develop and maintain an agency-wide information security programme that includes:

- Periodic assessments of risk.
- Security policies, plans, and procedures.
- Periodic testing and evaluation.
- Security awareness training to inform personnel.
- A security deficiency remediation programme.
- Incident detection, reporting, and response.
- Plans and procedures to ensure continuity of operations.

APPENDIX B

Threat Vectors

I n this Appendix we consider the effect on an organisation's security posture that stems from some of the opportunities and demands facing leaders today. Obviously, priorities for an organisation and in particular the Chief Information Officer (CIO) will change over time. This is not intended as either a fixed list of priorities or an exhaustive list of security considerations. It is intended instead as a catalyst for considering security implications and related activities when things change, and to encourage a proactive rather than reactive approach.

OUTSOURCING/OFFSHORING

Outsourcing has increasingly gained acceptance as a viable option for a wide variety of IT and business functions. Its benefits to an organisation can include improved cost management and potential savings, access to an increased skills base, and the opportunity for the business to focus on its core competencies. Increased interest in offshore outsourcing in particular has extended beyond the well-established and widely known market in India to low-cost markets around the globe.

Security Implications

- Increasing presence in the market of new players whose security expertise may be immature requires that organisations exercise robust and comprehensive due diligence before selecting a provider, and rigorous and regular audits afterwards.
- The difficulty of directing, managing, and monitoring what is not under one's own roof necessitates the effective use of contracts, service-level agreements, and rights to audit as well as the retention of suitable people to oversee the arrangement. It is important that contractual commercial factors are complemented by explicit requirements and monitoring of security and controls.
- Who's looking at your data? Employee vetting varies considerably between service providers, and stringent segregation of different organisations' systems and data is critical.
- The security provided for your systems and data should be dictated by your own organisation's threat assessment and the resultant security policies, not solely the provider's view.
- Political instability in other countries and risk of terrorism in any country means additional and rigorous consideration of physical security, employee vetting, controls that prevent exploitation through blackmail or bribery, and business continuity arrangements.
- Do not assume anything. Confirm for yourselves that the provider has the fundamentals—not just the technologies, but the people and processes as well—virus protection, network security, firewall protection, and business continuity arrangements.

COST MANAGEMENT

Cost management means different things to different organisations; additionally, the focus varies with the economic outlook. When businesses find themselves facing extremely challenging economic environments, they often impose severe cost-cutting demands and develop "survival plans" as their business plans. Many businesses have learned that even in stronger economic times, IT offers a number of cost-cutting opportunities. Astute organisations continue to seek them, particularly in operational areas, to fund investment for business change programmes.

Security Implications

- Cost cutting often involves loss or relocation of jobs, which in themselves have a number of security implications. These include damage done by disgruntled employees either from within or after leaving, and previously unknown "key person" reliance, that is, the recognition only after terminating the employment of an individual or group that the business-critical knowledge they held is now unavailable.
- A framework for cost-cutting decisions is needed to ensure dependencies are considered, and the degree to which IT controls may be reduced or security compromised. For example, failure to install an upgrade may result in security exposures that can be exploited by hackers, and project cuts may preclude the ability to comply with pending legislation.
- Justifying information security does not easily conform to typical investment return calculations such as ROI; however, it is important that value for spend disciplines are a key consideration in determining security investments.
- Procurement and IT departments may have different perspectives. Total Cost of Ownership (TCO) calculations vary according to the specific type of IT spend, the nature of which may not be fully understood by procurement departments.

- Beware of "hype," whether from media or vendors; there are many numbers available that claim to represent the cost of security incidents, potential cost savings, and so on.

GOVERNANCE

International regulation and legislation, such as Sarbanes-Oxley and Basel 2, as well as increased demand from industry regulators have put responsibility for implementing, testing, and demonstrating an effective control framework firmly on the board. Legislative changes and differences between individual country requirements have left many organisations struggling to understand compliance requirements (let alone implement them), particularly where cross-border activity takes place. These drivers can provide an opportunity for organisations to justify improvements in information security and control if they can clarify goals and priorities.

Security Implications

- Governance, regulation, and legislation compliance requires board-level drive and sponsorship, as well as cross-organisation input and commitment.
- Organisations need clarity about where the responsibility lies to avoid potential gaps in compliance.
- Countries have different compliance requirements and different legislation. Legislation in many countries is struggling to keep up with technology development, and cross-jurisdiction activity contributes to confusion in organisations.
- Keeping up to date with forthcoming regulatory and/or legislative requirements is *always* critical.
- A variety of standards and control frameworks, such as COBIT, COSO, and ISO 17799, exist to assist organisations in setting a standard to achieve effective IT control. In the absence of clarity or guidance to meet regulatory or legislative requirements, these frameworks provide sound standards.

TERRORISM

Increased occurrence of terrorist attack means increased consideration of physical security requirements and business continuity throughout the business and the full supply chain. A physical attack combined with a denial-of-service cyberattack could exponentially increase human casualties, social or economic disruption, and/or financial loss.

Security Implications

- Risk analysis should include threat and vulnerability relationships between business units and should be ongoing rather than periodic (for example, annual).
- Business continuity requirements need to be considered across the full supply chain and in conjunction with business priorities; for example, initiatives to reduce the number of suppliers may expose the business to over-reliance on individual suppliers, which can be a problem in the event of a supplier failure.
- Physical and logical security need to be considered together in the context of the whole business.
- Business priorities, recovery timescales, and dependencies need to be clear, agreed upon, and reviewed regularly.

NEW AND EVOLVING TECHNOLOGIES

Rapid development of new and evolving technologies, such as wireless, radio frequency identification (RFID), provides the opportunities to support business change. Security, however, remains a key consideration.

Security Implications

- New or evolving technologies often have untried or immature security; the security available needs to be balanced with business needs and benefit.

- Businesses should be aware of inconsistent, immature, flawed, or absent standards for evolving technologies.
- Introduction of new technologies need to be treated as programmes of change, with all the associated people and process issues taken into account.
- New technologies can introduce unanticipated concerns. For example, the introduction of RFID intended to provide enhanced efficiency in the supply chain and retail sectors has raised concerns with consumers about potential privacy implications.
- Security needs to be built in; as with any change, there are people and process considerations for security as well as technology.

DATA MANAGEMENT

Increasing demand for timely and comprehensive management information combined with new mechanisms for data storage present new considerations for security and control. Businesses need to think about the security of data in use, in transit, and at rest.

Security Implications

- Organisations need to be sure they know what data is being held and where; data held for development and testing purposes is relevant as well as that in live (production) systems.
- Data transfer rules and regulations are continually changing, as monitoring is needed.
- Data authentication, authorisation, and access to read, write, copy, or delete are all factors to be considered.
- Multiple data locations, third party access resulting from extended enterprise (such as outsourcers, suppliers, or customers), and the sheer volume of data mean greater consideration of how to protect and ensure data integrity.

MALWARE

The proliferation of viruses and worms, vastly increased speed of proliferation, new approaches such as "blended" attacks and the resulting high impact on business has forced the issue out of the IT/security arena and firmly onto the board's agenda. There is evidence and increasing concerns that criminals, virus writers, and hackers are working more closely together than ever before. This further increases the risk surrounding theft of bank and credit card details. Other activity shows hackers blackmailing online betting firms just before major sporting events with threats to destroy their network. It is important to remember that access to information on how to write and distribute viruses, as well as "how to hack" is widely available.

Security Implications

- Organisations need reliable sources of information about vulnerabilities, including trend monitoring.
- Priorities should be driven by good operational practice, not media hype.
- Security policies and procedures need to be enforced.
- Patch deployment approaches need to keep up with vulnerabilities.
- Employee awareness is critical; for example, instructions not to open certain attachments, guidance on distribution of e-mails and, most importantly, how to identify and avoid "social engineering" efforts are of utmost importance.
- Emergency response procedures need to be fit-for-purpose, tested, and up-to-date.

MOBILE WORKING

Business change and progress in technology to support mobile working has increased moves towards a mobile workforce; this means that more people work from home or have connectivity when out "in the field," working from other offices, or when in transit, such as at airports. Indeed, some organisations are progressing toward an open platform built solely on generic, publicly available services, hardware, software, and support.

Security Implications

- For business-supported infrastructures, there are difficulties of software distribution (for example, virus updates and patch management) when people are out of the office for lengthy periods.
- For businesses reliant on public infrastructures, there are difficulties in ensuring that employees are practicing safe computing so as to protect their colleagues and the organisation.
- There is potential for less control over what people are doing, the extent to which they are aware of policies and procedures, and the extent to which they comply with them.
- Decisions about standards become difficult when employee demand is ahead of corporate decision making; for example, demand from users for PDAs caught many organisations unaware. Decisions had not yet been made about hardware/software standards or security policies.
- For mobile working to be of real value, mobile users need access to their corporate applications and information. This scenario is fraught with authentication issues; it is important to consider where these corporate systems and data are located.
- As theft or loss is a significant risk, the importance of protected data is critical.

MERGERS, ACQUISITIONS, AND ALLIANCES

Continued interest and activity in the merger and acquisition arena often focuses on the financial due diligence of the transactions without due consideration of IT security and control issues.

Security Implications

- Rigorous technical due diligence needs to be carried out alongside financial due diligence in order to identify potential security issues or high-remediation cost acquisitions.

- IT contracts create exposures due to steep exit or transfer clauses that limit opportunities to gain business or cost efficiencies.
- Security weaknesses in acquired systems or incompatibility with existing systems leave organisations vulnerable to errors, irregularities, and fraud.
- IT centres based in geographically remote areas may need to comply with different laws, and IT contracts may be country-specific.
- Absent or incomplete IT asset inventory of resources obtained can result in licensing or shrinkage issues, due to the lack of knowledge about what assets should actually exist.
- Insider trading opportunities exist for all involved parties if security of the transaction is not maintained.

PERFORMANCE MANAGEMENT AND REPORTING

The ways of doing business are changing, and there is a proliferation of means to collect and analyse data. This has increased demand for real-time management and performance information, often referred to as management dashboards or scorecards.

Security Implications

- A key challenge is determining which stakeholders require information and why.
- Another challenge for security is determining what needs to be reported and what information is available.
- The balance between the cost of collecting the data for dashboards versus its value needs to be considered.

APPENDIX C

Ernst & Young
2004 Digital Security Overview

An Executive Guide and Diagnostic

For the first edition of this book, Ernst & Young surveyed major North American organisations to determine the state of digital security readiness in some of the world's largest organisations. For this second edition of the book, we extended the survey to a number of countries across the globe in addition to surveying organisations in the United States.

Our aim was to understand the current state of digital security readiness and identify changes since the original survey carried out in April 2002.[1] We therefore conducted interviews with respondents in 24 countries including North America, Europe, Scandinavia, South Africa, the Middle East, and the Far East. We interviewed senior decision-makers on information security in a variety of industry sectors amongst the largest organisations in each country.

Our interviews covered the nine security agenda components introduced in Chapter 4, specifically:

- IT Policies, Standards, and Guidelines.
- Intrusion Detection.
- Incident Response.
- Privacy.
- Physical Security.
- Asset and Service Management.
- Vulnerability Management.
- Entitlement Management.
- Business Continuity.

For each of these items, this chapter presents:

- Survey results.
- Implications of those results.
- Questions to ask of your own organisation.

THE HEADLINES

As expected, there is some good news:

- *Information security policies*—83 percent of respondents have a documented information security policy.
- *Business alignment*—85 percent of respondents undertake reviews of information security policy for consistency with current business processes and risk strategy.
- *Privacy policies*—89 percent of respondents have addressed this area.
- *Physical security policies*—88 percent of respondents have a policy in place.

However, at least one-fifth of organisations are missing some fundamentals:

- Twenty percent of respondents have no intrusion detection system.
- Over 30 percent of organisations surveyed do not have a documented incident-response plan or have only a document showing who to call in the event of an incident.

Some further sobering news:

- Only 25 percent of those respondents with a security policy confirmed their policies were supported by documented procedures/guidelines and were implemented and followed.
- Thirty-three percent of those with a business continuity/recovery plan do not have a method for testing it.
- Thirty-nine percent of respondents do not train their employees in physical security.

Indications are that activity is taking place in many areas, but organisations are making some fundamental mistakes in not following through on the initial activities of policy setting and plan development, and in particular, lack activity on:

- Recognising the role of people in addition to process and technology.
- Testing plans to make sure they are effective.
- Ensuring compliance with policies.

These activities are fundamental to ensuring the investment is worthwhile and effectively meets business needs.

There are also indications that key business decisions may be being left to IT alone:

- Fourteen percent of respondents indicated that in the event of an incident, they had no formal process that required executive level involvement.
- A further 21 percent left the decision to involve company executives about the incident to the computer security incident-response team leader.

- Thirty-seven percent of respondents said that only the security department is formally trained in security measures.

The real concern is that organisations may be deluding themselves with a false sense of security because the information provided to them makes it appear as though things are better than they really are. In addition, organisations are not asking the right questions.

For example, the phrase "We have a business continuity plan" sounds good, but "We are one of the 33 percent of organisations who have no method for testing our plan" or "We are one of the 15 percent of organisations who haven't tested our plan" might be more accurate. "We have a documented information security policy" might also sound good, whereas "We don't know if unauthorised people are trying to access our system because we are one of the 20 percent of organisations without an Intrusion Detection System" might indicate the real state of digital security.

Global Variations

The state of readiness for digital security incidents varies by region and by individual aspect. According to their responses, respondents in the Americas, particularly North America, appear to be better prepared than those in other regions in that they are more likely to have:

- A complete incident-response plan (40 percent in North America compared to 22 percent elsewhere).
- Privacy policies in place (71 percent compared to 58 percent).
- Fully automated asset monitoring (33 percent compared to 22 percent).

Meanwhile, although Far East respondents are just as likely as those in North America to have business continuity plans enabling them to recover their entire enterprise, in many other areas they appear to lag behind the other regions, most notably on:

- Having privacy policies in place (52 percent in the Far East compared to 65 percent elsewhere).
- Having the ability to identify and track vulnerabilities (12 percent compared to 19 percent).

There is some correlation between areas of challenge and less-than-accepted practice. For example:

- Fifteen percent of those with written continuity/recovery plans have not yet tested them; this rises to 26 percent amongst those for whom business continuity is felt to be the foremost security challenge.
- Eighty-three percent of respondents have an information security policy; this drops to 74 percent amongst those for whom IT policies, standards, and guidelines comprise the foremost security challenge.

Sixty-two percent of respondents said that digital security functions report to the Head of IT or the IT department, although an encouraging 17 percent report to the Board.

Business continuity is considered to be the foremost security challenge overall, although in North America this is second to IT policies, standards, and guidelines.

Which one *of these do you consider to be your organisation's foremost security challenge?* (numbers are percentages of respondents)

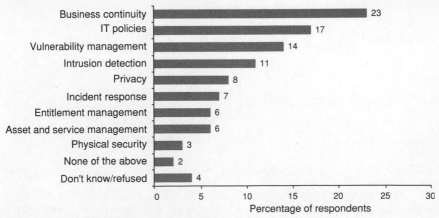

Note: Due to rounding, figures may not total 100.

IT POLICIES, STANDARDS, AND GUIDELINES—
IS YOUR SECURITY BUILT ON A SOLID FOUNDATION
OR A QUAGMIRE?

Organisations that (1) have in place comprehensive policies, standards, and guidelines that have been validated and (2) review and update them regularly can proactively plan, manage, and respond to information security risks, threats, and vulnerabilities. Digital security programmes need a policy development and implementation structure to provide the foundation for all other security-related activities. Such a structure provides a pivotal communication link between executive management, the digital security team, and others in the extended enterprise who need to include digital security in their day-to-day activities.

The Results

Which of the following most closely describes the way in which information security policy compliance is monitored and administered within your organisation? Is it . . . ?

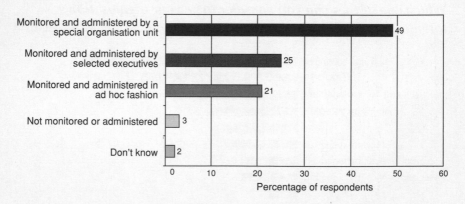

Documented policies. Eighty-three percent of respondents indicated they have a documented security policy, percentages being somewhat higher among those from the Americas and Scandinavia, and correspondingly lower among Middle East respondents. Industry differences indicated energy respondents falling below this percentage.

Business alignment. Eighty-five percent of respondents undertake reviews of policy for consistency with current business processes and risk strategy, percentages being similar across the world. Forty-three percent undertake these reviews annually, while 34 percent undertake reviews more frequently, 11 percent carrying out reviews monthly.

The percentage of North American organisations that review policies for consistency once a month has more than doubled since 2002 from 10 percent to 22 percent. Structured monitoring and administration of IT security policies have also increased.

One-fifth of global respondents in 2004 undertake the review process in an ad hoc fashion compared to 44 percent of respondents in the 2002 survey.

Does your company undertake reviews of its information security policies for consistency with current business processes and risk strategy? (see pie chart)

How often does your company review its information security policies? (see bar graph)

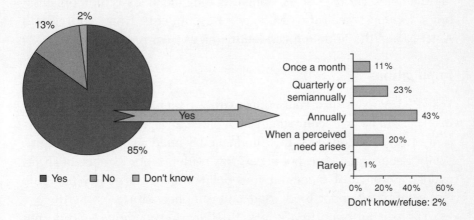

Fit with standards. Only 17 percent of those with a policy indicated that all necessary policies comply with domains defined by recognised models, such as ISO 1799, although a further 45 percent said that most necessary policies comply. However, only 25 percent of those respondents with a security policy confirmed that their policies were supported by documented procedures and guidelines, and were implemented and followed.

To what extent are your information security policies designed to cover the domains defined by recognised models such as ISO 17799, CISSP or common criteria?

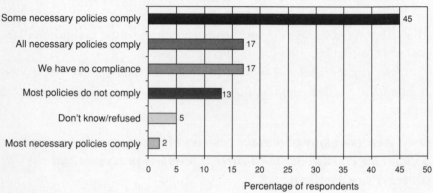

Note: Due to rounding, figures may not total 100.

How big is the challenge? Seventeen percent of respondents cited information security policies, standards and guidelines as their organisation's foremost security challenge. Respondents from both North America and the Middle East identified it as their top challenge.

Implications

While 83 percent of organisations with a documented security policy may seem to be an encouragingly high percentage, it means that 17 percent of organisations lack this fundamental building block of security. Whilst documentation is not necessarily evidence of existence in all situations, absence of a documented policy means the policy has little chance of being understood, used, and complied with.

There is an opportunity here for those respondents who do not seem to be making use of available standards to seize this opportunity to increase confidence in their policies and standards. Different models focus on different domains of security but most provide a good starting point and give confidence that there is a good baseline.

However, no matter how comprehensive policies are, they are of little use if they are not validated by the business, communicated, and translated into procedures and guidelines that are implemented and followed.

Questions to Ask

The following are important questions for an organisation to ask about its own information security policies:

- Are there documented information security policies, procedures and guidelines? Does everyone know about them, and do these policies flow through to provide minimum baseline standards for specific technologies?
- Have they been cross-checked against available and recognised models? Are there processes and mechanisms to ensure they remain consistent with business objectives and priorities, and include proactive validation?
- Is timely and regular education and training provided to make policies and procedures visible and help people understand, use, and comply with them? This should include user awareness and specialised training for the IT community.
- Is there visible and measurable top level sponsorship?
- Has an assurance and monitoring programme been implemented to ensure policies and procedures are being applied and complied with?

INCIDENT RESPONSE—WILL YOU BE READY WHEN THE WORST HAPPENS?

A security incident can be many things. Not all of them are malicious, and many may be the result of poor operational practices, lack of understanding, or simply carelessness—but all are potentially damaging. The actions of hackers and the impact of malware including viruses have been widely reported in the media. However, the more common and continual problems are not reported. These include policy violations, unauthorised use of networks or systems, attempts to gain unauthorised access to data or systems, and unauthorised attempts to change or delete information within a system. They also include employees who write down new passwords, then leave them taped to the front of their monitors; a former employee who retains access to systems; or a new employee who erroneously posts confidential data on a public Web site. All of these scenarios, and many more, can be classified as security incidents.

The Results

Which of these possible approaches to incident-response planning best describes your organisation's approach?

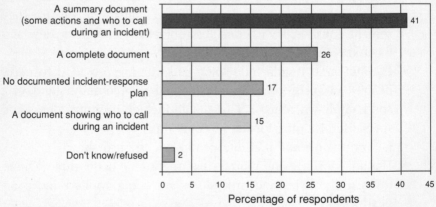

Note: Due to rounding, figures may not total 100.

Completeness. Just over one quarter of respondents believed they had a complete and documented approach to incident response, including the definition of an incident, threat alert categories and escalation procedures, roles and responsibilities, investigative steps, and system resumption strategies.

North American respondents did much better. Fifty percent of North American respondents fell into this category, an increase of 4 percent since the question was asked two years ago. Industry leaders in this area came from the technology communications and entertainment sector (40 percent), financial sector (37 percent), and energy (25 percent) sectors.

Forty-one percent of respondents have a document that outlines some actions and who to call in the event of an incident, and 15 percent have a document that shows only who to call in the event of an incident. Seventeen percent have no documented incident-response plan.

Only 7 percent of North American respondents fell into the category of "no documented incident-response plan," while 17 percent of European respondents, 30 percent of Middle East respondents, and 22 percent of Far East respondents gave this response.

Making business decisions. Fourteen percent of respondents said that in the event of an incident, they had no formal process that required executive level involvement, and a further 21 percent left the decision to involve company executives to the computer security incident-response team leader. Sixty-two percent of respondents informed either company-level or divisional-level managers who were then responsible for resulting business decisions.

Twenty percent of European respondents had no formal process requiring executive level involvement while only 7 percent of North American respondents fell into this category. Changes in North American responses from the 2002 survey showed a shift in who makes the business decisions. Twenty-two percent of North American respondents in 2002 left responsibility for resulting business decisions with the computer security incident-response team leader, while only 13 percent of North American respondents today leave them with this critical responsibility.

Fifty percent of Middle East respondents said they left business decisions to the security incident-response team while 15 percent of them had no formal process for requiring executive level involvement. The pharmaceutical, technology, communications and entertainment, and financial services sectors had a high level of respondents who said they would inform company or divisional managers, who would then be responsible for resulting business decisions.

How big is the challenge? Only 7 percent of respondents rated incident-response at their foremost security challenge.

Implications

Almost one third of organisations are likely to find themselves in a difficult situation in the event of an incident; the 15 percent of respondents with only a list of who to call are likely to find themselves little better off than the 17 percent who have no plan at all.

The good news on these results is that there appears to have been at least a shift towards recognition that business decisions following an incident cannot be left to the computer security incident-response team alone unless that team includes senior business representation. The time to make these decisions is not when an incident actually occurs.

A few years ago, many organisations felt there were so many types of incidents that may occur that it was pointless to develop a plan to address all scenarios. An increase in terrorism in recent years as well as an increase in virus incidents means that this belief cannot continue.

Questions to Ask

Following are important questions to ask about incident response:

- Is there an incident-response plan?
- Has it been challenged to see if it will meet business-specific needs based on threat analysis specific to the organisation? Remember: Incidents may limit physical access to buildings.
- Does the plan include all relevant people, including critical third parties?
- Is there a clear escalation path to ensure executive level involvement when an agreed "seriousness" threshold is reached?
- Has it been tested and the results acted upon? What other mechanisms exist to keep the plan up to date?
- What mechanisms exist to ensure sufficient coverage for people who are on leave, on training courses, or unexpectedly absent? What single points of failure are there in the plan, whether locations, equipment, or people?

PRIVACY—WHAT DO THE MYRIAD OF REGULATIONS REALLY MEAN?

Conducting business in a digitally-interconnected economy requires incorporating privacy safeguards into operations at all levels, particularly information systems. A few words may be helpful at this point to ensure a consistent understanding of what is meant by privacy. In general, privacy refers to an individual's right to control what information about them is revealed and to whom, as well as what others may do with that information. This right, however, is affected by laws and regulations as well as social considerations.

The degree to which an organisation chooses to adhere to increasingly stringent and complex privacy standards determines whether its privacy policies are primarily a competitive advantage or a potential risk. Organisations must balance the need to maximise the value of the private information they possess while building and maintaining trust and confidence among stakeholders. Privacy includes enterprise-wide controls and proactive countermeasures supported by formal policies to ensure that only authorised users gain access to private data.

The Results

Which of the following best describes your company's current attitude towards information privacy?

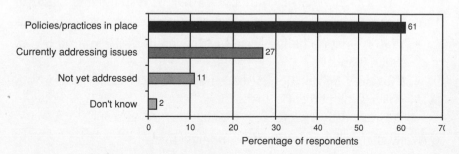

Note: Due to rounding, figures may not total 100.

Sixty-one percent of respondents currently have policies or practices in place that address information privacy, and 27 percent are addressing the issue. Only 11 percent of respondents said they have not yet addressed the issue.

The top reason given for addressing privacy by far is regulatory compliance; 53 percent of respondents cite this reason. Regulatory compliance was consistently the top reason across all countries and industry sectors. Risk management was cited by 20 percent, all other reasons achieving very low response rates, although competitive advantage and customer expectations found some support from respondents in a few individual countries.

What would you say is the primary reason that your company has addressed the issue of information privacy?

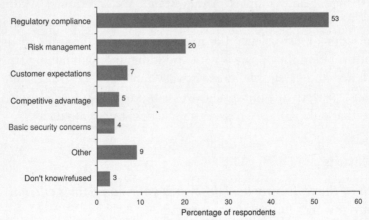

There was a high level of confidence (that is, respondents agree or strongly agree) that:

- Personal data is only released with consent or if required by law (89 percent).
- Customer information is shared only in accordance with privacy policies (81 percent).
- Personal data is protected from hackers (85 percent).

And only slightly lower levels of confidence that:

- Customer data is collected only in accordance with privacy policies (77 percent).

- Only authorised persons can access customer data (78 percent).
- The use of customer information by third parties complies with privacy policies (75 percent).

How big is the challenge? Only 8 percent of respondents rated privacy as their top concern.

Implications

Privacy seems to be receiving management attention, if only because organisations recognise the need to achieve compliance with legislative or regulatory requirements. Given the extensive publicity that privacy issues are receiving on a global basis, the confidence that organisations appear to have in this area must be challenged. One of the most well-publicised examples was JetBlue's decision to provide information on over one million passengers to U.S. authorities during the summer of 2002. This decision was followed by accusations of deceptive practices, a federal privacy investigation, and class action lawsuits. EU bodies have since expressed concern about attempts by U.S. government agencies to transfer airline passenger information to U.S. authorities. A resolution adopted by the European Parliament in March 2004 concluded that lack of resources and an unwillingness by national governments to enforce the directive has had an adverse effect on personal privacy. The resolution condemns member states for handing over to U.S. authorities details of passengers flying to the United States. The patchwork of laws, complex requirements, potentially conflicting international standards, changing rules, and heightened concerns about personal privacy and data-sharing practices have focused attention on liability issues.

Questions to Ask

The following are important questions to ask about privacy:

- Who is responsible for privacy in the organisation?
- Are privacy laws and legislation as they affect the organisation fully understood?

- Is there a consistent approach throughout the (extended) organisation?
- Are at least the most stringent requirements complied with?
- How is compliance with stated policies ensured wherever that data is held?
- Are the activities of business partners and other relevant third parties who hold critical business data being monitored?

INTRUSION DETECTION SYSTEMS—WHO'S TRYING TO GET AT YOUR SYSTEMS?

Knowing the identity of system users and the permissions they have been granted is a fundamental issue in systems administration. If there is no way of knowing who is allowed access to the system and what they are allowed to do, there is no way of knowing who does not belong there or who is engaging in suspicious behaviour. The ability to detect and isolate an intruder or an authorised user who has circumvented applied controls is a basic requirement of a digital security programme. It is not surprising, therefore, that most organisations consider the ability to detect and isolate an intrusion to be high priority.

The Results

Does your company have an IT Intrusion Detection System?

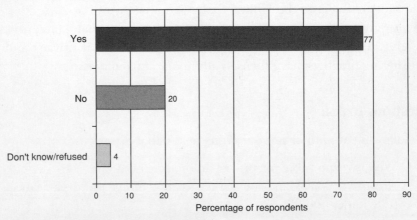

Note: Due to rounding, figures may not total 100.

Seventy-seven percent of respondents have an Intrusion Detection System (IDS); respondents in the technology, communication, and entertainment, and financial sectors scored highest at 87 percent and 85 percent, respectively.

Of those without an intrusion detection system, 21 percent responded that they actively monitor between 95 percent and 100 percent of their Internet and extranet connections for intrusions, and over 25 percent said they actively monitor 95 percent to 100 percent of critical servers for intrusion.

How big is the challenge? Eleven percent of respondents identified intrusion detection as their foremost security challenge, fourth overall in the list of challenges.

Implications

It would be very difficult for most organisations without intrusion detections systems to monitor Internet and extranet connections effectively. Most organisations simply do not have the resources to check them effectively. Even for those with an IDS, lack of deployment throughout the business, deficient design or configuration, insufficient testing, or lack of resources to monitor or maintain it all limit the system's effectiveness. Well-designed and well-implemented Intrusion Detection Systems can provide heightened visibility of threats that face the organisation; their effectiveness, however, needs to be viewed in the context of other security measures. Shareholders and other stakeholders expect an organisation to take reasonable steps to protect its resources and are likely to be unforgiving in the event of an incident if it were to prove that reasonable steps had not been taken.

Questions to Ask

The following are important questions to ask about intrusion detection:

- Is there an intrusion prevention strategy?
- Is there an Intrusion Detection System?
- If not, how is activity inside and outside the network monitored? (Reliance on system logs is not usually a satisfactory option; most organisations do not have the resources to check them effectively).

- What percentage of the network does monitoring cover (for example, critical servers only, a percentage of Internet and extranet connections, and so on)? What is the reasoning behind the decision?
- Are sufficient resources allocated to implement, monitor, and maintain intrusion detection effectively?
- Has the intrusion detection device been tested to ensure it is configured correctly to provide the protection levels required ? How often is it tested?

PHYSICAL SECURITY—WHO IS ON YOUR PREMISES AND WHAT ARE THEY DOING?

Physical measures, such as locks, bars, alarms, and uniformed guards, are fundamental to an organisation's total security effort because they are key components of controlling access to digital assets. In a digital security programme, physical security efforts are in alignment with proactive, enterprise-wide digital security operations. An organisation that ignores the physical aspect of digital security is leaving a significant vulnerability unaddressed.

The Results

Which of the following areas does your organisation's physical security policy address?

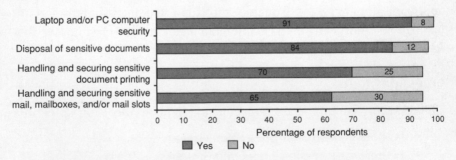

Eighty-six percent of respondents have a physical security policy in place. There has been an increase since 2002 in those respondents who include laptop and PC security as well as disposal of sensitive documents (84 percent compared to 80 percent) in their policies. Ninety-one percent of 2004 organisations indicated their physical security policies cover laptop and/or PC computer security compared to 85 percent in the 2002 survey and responses are generally consistently high across the globe.

Eighty-eight percent of North American respondents say their physical security policy now covers disposal of sensitive documents compared to 80 percent in 2002, a response perhaps to high-profile corporate failures in which the disposal (or otherwise) of documents received significant publicity.

Communication of physical security policies is less impressive. Only 58 percent of respondents provide training in physical security and of these, nearly one-fifth do not train new staff. Just over half of respondents provide annual security awareness training while 74 percent say they send periodic e-mails about security. Thirty-seven percent of respondents said that only the security department is formally trained in security measures.

How big is the challenge? Only 3 percent of respondents rated physical security as their foremost security challenge, scoring the lowest of all the challenges, indicating perhaps that most organisations at least understand what needs to be done.

Implications

The existence of physical security policies and the increased inclusion of elements such as laptops is encouraging. Setting standards and defining respective company and employee responsibilities is at least a starting point.

The limited level of communication of these policies is disappointing but, more than that, there is a significant risk of management's having misplaced confidence in their security measures. If policies are developed but not communicated effectively, there is limited chance of them being applied. Further, while e-mail is a widespread method of communication, it is likely to prove less than effective as the sole method for raising security awareness.

Protecting employees and company assets is of increasing priority for senior management, which means a fully deployed, enterprise-wide physical security approach must be a critical component of any digital security programme.

Questions to Ask

The following are important questions to ask about physical security:

- Is the physical security policy integrated with other relevant policies in the organisation?
- How it is it kept up to date, including proactive consideration of new threats, business, and technology changes?
- Is there a communication plan for all relevant personnel, including training for new staff, contractors, and relevant third parties? Is it followed up with regular awareness sessions? Are there innovative and creative communication mechanisms? (E-mails may not be the best).
- Is senior management really leading by example?
- How is compliance regularly measured and monitored? Are the results of compliance reviews acted upon?

ASSET AND SERVICE MANAGEMENT—ARE YOU SURE YOU KNOW WHERE YOUR ASSETS ARE?

One of the goals of asset and service management is increased productivity. Mechanisms, procedures, and technologies that might improve productivity are measured in terms of potential utility and return on investment. It is difficult to dispute that knowing what assets are owned and where they are is highly useful knowledge to any organisation, and that properly managing the assets' deployment and use carries with it a return on investment. Having in place streamlined mechanisms, such as fully-automated asset tracking systems and automatically deployed application and system upgrades, can secure that return. Assets that are overlooked can be problematic by becoming a breeding ground for vulnerabilities.

The Results

Which of the following statements best describes your organisation's approach to monitoring physical IT assets?

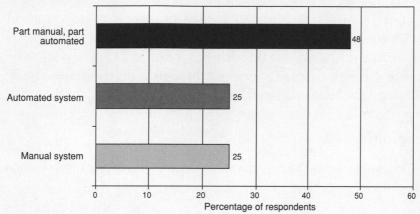

Note: Due to rounding, figures may not total 100.

The proportion of organisations using either fully automated or fully manual systems is evenly split at 25 percent each, with 48 percent of organisations using partially automated and partially manual systems. Of those respondents who are not using fully automated systems, just over 50 percent provide software upgrades and release automatically through the network. Thirty-two percent of organisations install software upgrades on a person-by-person basis while 14 percent use support staff to install software upgrades per department.

In addition, of those respondents who are not using a fully auto-mated system, only 16 percent are making use of a comprehensive asset management package and a further 30 percent use a package to record some, but not all, information.

How big is the challenge? Only 6 percent of respondents rated asset and service management as their foremost security challenge.

Implications

It is likely that those organisations not making full use of automated asset management systems are sacrificing efficiency, accuracy, or both.

Effective asset management is about more than just maintaining equipment inventories and software licensing documentation, although
managing these effectively contributes to sound cost management.
Unidentified assets can contribute to an organisation's vulnerabilities.
A properly designed and implemented asset and service management
solution should include assets throughout the enterprise.

Clear accountability for the activities in the asset and service management life cycle, from procurement through to retirement, is crucial,
including those assets managed by third parties.

Questions to Ask

The following are important questions to ask about asset and service
management:

- Is the approach to asset and service management effective in providing an accurate and up-to-date picture?
- Is there clarity about accountabilities for asset and service management throughout the enterprise?
- How effective is it in providing information to support calculations such as Total Cost of Ownership (TCO) or Return on
  Investment (ROI)?

VULNERABILITY MANAGEMENT—DO YOU REALLY KNOW WHERE YOU ARE VULNERABLE?

Digital vulnerabilities and subsequent exploitations are constants in a
digitally-connected marketplace. They are difficult to discover and difficult to track, and therefore pose a huge, often hidden threat to the
integrity of information systems. The only way to effectively address
vulnerabilities is with a proactive, enterprise-wide methodology. Vulnerability management provides organisations with an integrated approach for centralised monitoring and automated methods of ensuring
that compliance and secure configurations are maintained throughout
the organisation. This can result in an improved security profile and significant cost savings.

The Results

Which of the following would best describe how effectively your organisation manages system vulnerability?

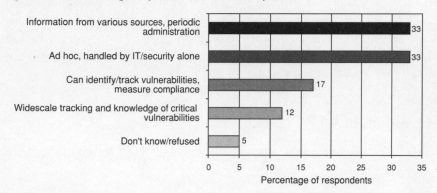

Percentage of respondents

Twenty-nine percent of respondents can identify and track vulnerabilities, measure compliance (or at least carry out widescale tracking), and have knowledge of critical vulnerabilities. Thirty-three percent gather information from various sources and carry out periodic administration, while a further 33 percent carry it out in an ad hoc fashion, leaving it to IT/Security alone. With regard to the frequency of assessing for vulnerabilities, 18 percent assess daily, a further 10 percent weekly, and a further 16 percent monthly. Twenty-nine percent of organisations assessed for known IT system vulnerabilities only when required and not on a regular basis, while 12 percent assessed only annually.

How big is the challenge? Fourteen percent of organisations identified it as their top challenge, third overall in the list of challenges.

Implications

There are a number of sources from which to obtain vulnerability information. There have been increasing efforts between software companies to formalise their efforts to provide consistent information and to potentially support the creation of a centralised resource. Symantec reports that there are 70 new vulnerabilities every week and 15 new viruses reported each day.[2] Given this volume, it seems many respondents are exposing themselves to significant risks.

The other challenge for organisations is the issue of patch management. There is much publicity about the exploitation of vulnerabilities for which patches have been made available, yet not deployed by organisations that subsequently fall victim. While patches may be made available to address vulnerabilities, they may bring reduced functionality, and organisations need to formalise their approach to patch management, including risk assessment and testing, as part of an overall vulnerability management activity.

Questions to Ask

The following are important questions to ask about vulnerability management:

- Who is responsible for vulnerability management?
- How often is an assessment for vulnerabilities made and is this often enough?
- Are external services used effectively to ensure validated and relevant information is being received?
- What is the approach to patch management? How is the need to test patches before applying them balanced with the need to apply patches rapidly (before they can be exploited)?
- Is there a clear understanding of vulnerabilities and threats and an integrated response in place?

ENTITLEMENT MANAGEMENT—WHO HAS ACCESS TO YOUR SYSTEMS? ARE THEY SUPPOSED TO BE THERE AND DO YOU KNOW WHAT THEY ARE DOING?

The success and security of a digital enterprise relies on trust as a basic requirement in any digital transaction. Customers entrust an organisation with private information, believing that the organisation has in place effective, enterprise-wide safeguards that have been validated and are ongoing. Managers must trust their employees to handle private information appropriately and apply the available safeguards. Executive management trusts that digital security decisions are aligned with business objectives and that they support and enable enhanced productivity and performance.

Establishing trust in a digital environment requires the use of controls that allow, restrict, and monitor access to information and systems. Such controls can include user authorisation and authentication systems, intrusion detection systems, smartcards, digital certificates, and biometrics, as well as many other devices and applications.

The Results

Which of these security solutions is currently deployed or planned for deployment over the next 12 to 18 months?

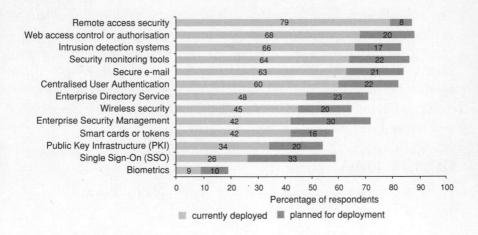

The top security solutions currently deployed are remote access security, Web access control or authorisation and intrusion detection systems, all deployed by over 65 percent of organisations. Top security solutions being considered are Single Sign-On (SSO) and Enterprise Security Management, both being considered by at least 30 percent of respondents. Over 20 percent of respondents are considering security monitoring tools, secure e-mail, centralised user authentication, and enterprise directory services within the next 12 to 18 months.

Of all the technologies discussed in the survey, biometrics scored lowest overall, implemented by 9 percent of respondents, and being considered by a further 10 percent. Three quarters of respondents said biometrics was not planned for deployment within 12 to 18 months. Other solutions identified by respondents as not planned for deployment were Smartcards and Tokens, identified by 40 percent, Single Sign-On (SSO) (37 percent), and Public Key Infrastructure (PKI) (36 percent).

Risk management is usually the primary driver for implementing new security solutions but determining the best security solution for a given situation depends on a variety of factors.

How big is the challenge? Only 6 percent of respondents rated entitlement management as their foremost security challenge.

Implications

The area of entitlement management is one where significant numbers of technologies are available to support organisations, and increasingly, leading software companies are taking an enterprise-wide view. The issue is not that organisations should be using one technology over another but that they have taken a holistic view of the organisation's needs and have mechanisms for the regular and proactive assessment of new technologies and capabilities.

Questions to Ask

The following are important questions to ask about entitlement management:

- Is there an enterprise-wide view of entitlement management? Is it clear where entitlement management takes place in the organisation? In most organisations, responsibilities are spread across a number of locations and/or functions.
- Is the business able to articulate its entitlement needs?
- What is the approach to identifying and selecting technologies to support entitlement management?
- How does the organisation keep up-to-date with new and evolving technologies and solutions to assess their abilities to meet business needs?

- How effective is the process for achieving regular revalidation of entitlement from business owners of applications and data?

BUSINESS CONTINUITY—ARE YOU REALLY SURE YOUR BUSINESS CONTINUITY PLANS WOULD KEEP YOUR BUSINESS GOING IF THE WORST HAPPENS?

No one likes to think about disasters, but, natural or deliberate, physical or logical, they happen. In today's digitally-interconnected world, threats can appear unexpectedly and an unprepared organisation can be seriously compromised before the incident has been detected. The losses in terms of downtime and damage to brand and corporate image can be staggering. This is why it is vital that every organisation has the ability to recover quickly and cost-effectively, and restore critical systems, processes, and data. Organisations must have the ability to rapidly deploy personnel, processes, and technology to support the recovery of business operations and information systems.

The Results

Which of the following would you consider to be your primary means of ensuring that your business continuity or disaster recovery plans are current?

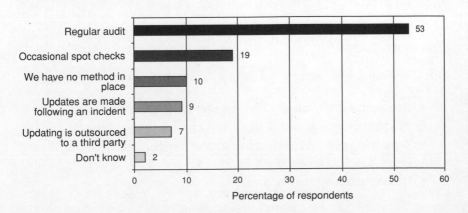

Only 20 percent of respondents believed they had developed integrated plans for recovering the entire enterprise. Twenty-two percent of North American organisations had an integrated plan, up from only 13 percent in 2002. Nine percent have plans for recovering critical business processes only, and 27 percent have plans for recovering mission critical systems and data only. More worryingly, 33 percent of organisations do not have plans in place for testing their business continuity or disaster recovery plans. Fifteen percent of organisations had not tested their plan at all and a further 9 percent had not tested their plan in the last year; these percentages are fairly spread across most of the countries.

How big is the challenge? Twenty-three percent of organisations identified business continuity as their foremost challenge—the top challenge overall.

Implications

It is encouraging that only 4 percent of organisations have no documented plans in place at all. Other responses, however, indicate some potential gaps in recovery plans, for example, organisations having plans to recover some critical business processes only. Approaches to testing also gave some cause for concern. While it is critical to update business continuity plans after an incident, it is not on its own an effective way of ensuring plans are current, nor are occasional spot checks unless used to supplement other activities such as regular reviews or tests.

Questions to Ask

The following are important questions to ask about business continuity:

- Are business continuity and disaster recovery plans in place?
- Are they relevant and do they work?
- Who was involved in developing them? (Business continuity is a cross-business issue.)
- When were they last tested?

- What were the results of that test and have the gaps been addressed?

IN CONCLUSION

Ask the right questions, challenge the answers, look for evidence, and measure the results.

Be clear where accountability lies for information security; there may be multiple stakeholders, but accountability can only lie in one place.

Effective information security must be directed and coordinated at the Board level, and directly relevant to your business.

DIGITAL SECURITY OVERVIEW
SELF-SCORING DIAGNOSTIC TOOL

An organisation's ability to defend itself must be proven before an event to know that those defences will hold during an event. This means there must be a programme in place to provide that defence, and that programme must be tailored to the unique needs and situation of the organisation.

The following tool enables executives to do two things: determine their organisation's ability to defend against an attack, and compare their organisation to industry peers to determine if theirs would be among the organisations able to survive if an industry-wide attack occurred. This systematic assessment can assist executives in understanding where the organisation's strengths and weaknesses are, and why they exist. The questions are based on those used in both the Ernst & Young 2002 and 2004 Digital Security Surveys. The questions in this tool have been weighted to enable self-scoring according to the Characteristics and Agenda Items of an effective digital security programme.

Instructions: Apply the scores indicated for each answer, following any question-specific directions noted in the shaded boxes. Both Agenda Item and Characteristic should be scored if a Characteristic is noted in the Scoring Box for that question. Please note: *Not all answers are weighted for scoring Characteristics.* Please see Chapter 2 for descriptions of the characteristics. The highest possible aggregate score is 75; the highest possible score on the Agenda Items is 45; and the highest possible score for Characteristics is 30.

Security Agenda Item: Intrusion Detection

1. Does your company have an Intrusion Detection System?

a) ☐ Yes.	2.00		
b) ☐ No.	0.00		
		Agenda Item	Characteristic: (None)
	Score		0

2. What percentage of your Internet and Extranet connections are actively monitored for intrusions?

a) <25%.	0.00		
b) 25%–50%.	0.50		
c) 50%–75%.	1.00		
d) 75%–95%.	1.50		
e) 95%–100%.	2.00		
		Agenda Item	Characteristic: (Proactive)
	Score		

3. What percentage of your critical servers are actively monitored for intrusions?

a) <25%.	0.00		
b) 25%–50%.	0.25		
c) 50%–75%.	0.50		
d) 75%–95%.	0.75		
e) 95%–100%.	1.00		
		Agenda Item	Characteristic: (Enterprise-wide)
	Score		

Intrusion Detection Subtotal		
Characteristic Subtotal		
Digital Security Overview Subtotal		

Security Agenda Item: Incident Response

4. Which one of the following best characterises how your organisation mitigates internal threats within your networks?

	Agenda Item	Characteristic: (Continuous)
a) Acceptable-use policies and procedures have been established and explained to employees. 0.50 b) Incident response policies and procedures have been developed. 0.75 c) Routine monitoring of employees for misconduct and inappropriate Internet usage. 1.00 d) No measures exist. 0.00		
Score		

5. Which of the following would be contacted if your company experienced a major virus problem, an unauthorised network intrusion, or a disclosure of sensitive information on the Internet?

Select all that apply:

	Agenda Item	Characteristic: (Continuous)
a) ☐ Internal computer security incident team. 1.00 b) ☐ An outside vendor that provides computer security incident response. 0.75 c) ☐ The internet service provider (ISP) who advises when network intrusion incidents occur. 0.50 d) ☐ Law enforcement. 0.25 e) ☐ Unsure. 0.00		
(Do not add values; assign highest score.)		
Score		

6. Which of the following best characterises the level of detail that is provided in your organisation's Incident-Response Plan?

	Agenda Item	Characteristic: (Formal)
a) It is a complete document that defines an incident, documents threat alert categories and escalation procedures, details roles and responsibilities, and contains incident scenarios, investigative steps, and system resumption strategies. 2.00 b) It is a summary document that outlines some actions and who to call during an incident. 1.50 c) It is a call list (phone tree). 1.00 d) The organisation does not have an IRP. 0.00 e) Unsure. 0.00		
Score		

7. Which of the following statements would you say best describes the level of executive involvement in computer security incidents?

a) Company officers are informed of incidents and are responsible for any resulting business decisions.		1.00
b) Division-level managers are informed of incidents and are responsible for any resulting business decisions.		0.75
c) The computer security incident response team leader is informed of incidents and is responsible for any resulting business decisions.		0.50
d) No formal process exists that requires executive-level involvement.		0.00

	Agenda Item	Characteristic: (Formal)
Score		

Incident Response Subtotal	
Characteristic Subtotal	
Digital Security Overview Running Subtotal	

Security Agenda Item: Privacy

8. On a scale of 1 to 5, with 1 being very confident and 5 being unconfident, where would you place your firm with regard to the following privacy practices?

Address all:		
a) ☐ We only collect customer's information in accordance with privacy policies. (Aligned) 1 *(0.50)*, 2 *(0.50)*, 3 *(0.25)*, 4 *(0.25)*, 5 *(0.00)*, Don't know *(0.00)*		
b) ☐ We only use or share customer information in accordance with privacy policies. (Aligned) 1 *(0.50)*, 2 *(0.50)*, 3 *(0.25)*, 4 *(0.25)*, 5 *(0.00)*, Don't know *(0.00)*		
c) ☐ We have internal controls and procedures to ensure only authorized persons can access customer data. (Aligned) 1 *(0.50)*, 2 *(0.50)*, 3 *(0.25)*, 4 *(0.25)*, 5 *(0.00)*, Don't know *(0.00)*		
d) ☐ Security procedures are in place to protect personal data from outside hackers or intruders. (Formal) 1 *(0.50)*, 2 *(0.50)*, 3 *(0.25)*, 4 *(0.25)*, 5 *(0.00)*, Don't know *(0.00)*		
e) ☐ We do not release customers' personal data to third parties without the express consent of the consumer or if required by law. (Aligned) 1 *(0.50)*, 2 *(0.50)*, 3 *(0.25)*, 4 *(0.25)*, 5 *(0.00)*, Don't know *(0.00)*		
f) ☐ We ensure the use of customer information by 3rd parties complies with the privacy policies. (Aligned) 1 *(0.50)*, 2 *(0.50)*, 3 *(0.25)*, 4 *(0.25)*, 5 *(0.00)*, Don't know *(0.00)*		

(Add all values to ascertain score.)	Agenda Item	Characteristic: (Aligned/Formal)
Score		

9. Have you completed or are you implementing or assessing the following privacy initiatives? Alternatively, do you consider them unnecessary?

Address all:

a) ☐ Privacy notice on company's homepage communicating company's online privacy practices. (Formal)

   Completed *(0.25)*, Implementing *(0.25)*, Assessing *(0.00)*, Unnecessary *(0. 00)*   ☐

b) ☐ Privacy notice communicating company's privacy policy for all offline uses of consumer data. (Formal)

   Completed *(0.25)*, Implementing *(0.25)*, Assessing *(0. 00)*, Unnecessary *(0. 00)*   ☐

c) ☐ Privacy notice communicating company's employee privacy practices. (None)

   Completed *(0.25)*, Implementing *(0.25)*, Assessing *(0. 00)*, Unnecessary *(0. 00)*   ☐

d) ☐ Privacy Seal from privacy-seal organisations (e.g., TRUSTe or BBBOnline) posted on company's homepage. (Validated)

   Completed *(0.25)*, Implementing *(0.25)*, Assessing *(0. 00)*, Unnecessary *(0. 00)*   ☐

e) ☐ Appoint Chief Privacy Officer. (None)

   Completed *(0.25)*, Implementing *(0.25)*, Assessing *(0. 00)*, Unnecessary *(0. 00)*   ☐

f) ☐ Privacy dispute resolution programme. (Aligned)

   Completed *(0.25)*, Implementing *(0.25)*, Assessing *(0.00)*, Unnecessary *(0. 00)*   ☐

g) ☐ Belong to association that is founded on complying with a set of privacy standards. (Aligned)

   Completed *(0.25)*, Implementing *(0.25)*, Assessing *(0. 00)*, Unnecessary *(0. 00)*   ☐

h) ☐ Independent auditing firm report verifying company is following its privacy policy. (Validated)

   Completed *(0.25)*, Implementing *(0.25)*, Assessing *(0. 00)*, Unnecessary *(0. 00)*   ☐

(Add all values to ascertain score.)	Agenda Item	Characteristic: (Formal, Validated, Aligned)
Score		

Privacy Subtotal	
Characteristic Subtotal	
Digital Security Overview Running Subtotal	

Security Agenda Item: Policies, Standards, and Guidelines

10. Which of the following are addressed by your organisation's IT security plan?

Select all that apply:

a) ☐ Documents roles and responsibilities/Formal reviews of security controls.		0.125
b) ☐ Information classification and destruction.		0.125
c) ☐ Personnel security and security awareness training.		0.125
d) ☐ Physical and environmental protection.		0.125
e) ☐ Business continuity planning.		0.125
f) ☐ Incident response planning.		0.125
g) ☐ Hardware and systems software maintenance controls/Application software maintenance controls.		0.125
h) ☐ Technical controls (identification, authentication, logical access controls, public access controls).		0.125
(Add all values to ascertain score.)	**Agenda Item**	**Characteristic: (Validated)**
Score		

11. How frequently are your information security policies reviewed for consistency with current business processes and risk strategy?

a) Once a month.	1.00	
b) Quarterly or semiannually.	0.75	
c) Annually.	0.50	
d) When a perceived need arises.	0.25	
e) Rarely/Never.	0.00	
	Agenda Item	**Characteristic: (Aligned)**
Score		

12. To what degree are your information security policies designed to cover the domains defined by ISO 17799, CISSP, Common Criteria, or another recognised model?

a) All necessary policies comply.	1.00	
b) Most necessary policies comply.	0.75	
c) Some necessary policies comply.	0.50	
d) Most policies do not comply.	0.25	
e) No compliance.	0.00	
	Agenda Item	**Characteristic: (Validated)**
Score		

13. How would you characterise your organisation's information security policies with regard to being universally deployed, monitored, and administered across the entire organisation?

a) We have attempted universal deployment with no administration/ monitoring of policies.	0.00	
b) We have attempted universal deployment with some administration/ monitoring of policies.	0.25	
c) We have achieved successful and complete universal monitoring/deployment/ administration of policies.	0.50	
d) We have made no attempt at universal deployment.	0.00	
	Agenda Item	**Characteristic: (Enterprise-wide)**
Score		

14. How would you characterise your information security policies with regard to being supported by documented procedures and guidelines for all users?

	Agenda Item	Characteristic: (Aligned)
a) They are documented, implemented, and followed. — 1.00		
b) They are documented; some implemented and followed. — 0.75		
c) They are documented; not implemented or followed. — 0.50		
d) Some documented, implemented, and followed. — 0.25		
e) They are not documented. — 0.00		
Score		

15. How is policy compliance monitored and administered within your organisation?

	Agenda Item	Characteristic: (Validated)
a) It is monitored and administered by a special organisational unit. — 0.50		
b) It is monitored and administered by selected executives. — 0.25		
c) It is monitored and administrated in ad hoc fashion. — 0.00		
d) It is not monitored or administered. — 0.00		
Score		

Policies, Standards, and Guidelines Subtotal	
Characteristic Subtotal	
Digital Security Overview Running Subtotal	

Security Agenda Item: Physical Security

16. Which of the following areas are addressed by your organisation's physical security policy?

Address all:

			Agenda Item	Characteristic: (Enterprise-wide)
a) Laptop/PC computer security.	☐ Yes *(.625)*	☐ No *(0.00)*		
b) Handling and securing sensitive document printing.	☐ Yes *(.625)*	☐ No *(0.00)*		
c) Handling and securing sensitive mail/mailboxes/mail slots.	☐ Yes *(.625)*	☐ No *(0.00)*		
d) Disposal of sensitive documents.	☐ Yes *(.625)*	☐ No *(0.00)*		
e) We have no physical security policy.	☐ Yes *(0.00)*	☐ No *(0.00)*		
(Add all values to ascertain score.)				
Score				

17. How often do your employees receive training on physical security measures?

a) New hire training.		1.00
b) Annual security awareness training.		2.50
c) Periodic e-mails about security.		1.00
d) Only the security department is formally trained in physical security measures.		1.00
e) No training or e-mailed updates offered.		0.00
(Do not add values; assign highest score.)	**Agenda Item**	**Characteristic: (None)**
Score		

Physical Security Subtotal	
Characteristic Subtotal	
Digital Security Overview Running Subtotal	

Security Agenda Item: Asset Management

18. Which one of the following statements best describes the way your organisation currently tracks physical assets?

a) Manually, using a spreadsheet or document to track changes, moves, disposal of assets, and physical inventory.		0.00
b) Automatically, using asset management software to track assets and associated costs.		1.00
c) Partially automated, partially manual.		0.50
d) We do not track physical assets.		0.00
	Agenda Item	**Characteristic: (Continuous)**
Score		

19. Which one of the following statements best describes the way workstation and desktop software upgrades/releases are deployed in your organisation (operating system and application upgrades)?

a) Support staff installs software upgrades on an "as needed" basis.		1.00
b) Support staff installs software upgrades per department.		1.00
c) Employees receive automatic upgrades through the network.		2.00
d) Our organisation seldom, if ever, upgrades software.		0.00
	Agenda Item	**Characteristic: (None)**
Score		

20. How does your organisation inventory the number of PCs in use, types/versions of PC software, available PC disk space, and network IP addresses?

a) The organisation uses a comprehensive asset management software package.		2.00
b) The organisation uses a software package that inventories some information, but not all asset information.		1.50
c) The organisation uses support staff to load software and maintain network information.		1.00
d) The organisation uses IT staff to manage network resources and audit PCs for licensed and authorised software.		0.50
e) Other.		0.00

	Agenda Item	Characteristic: (None)
Score		

Asset and Service Management Subtotal	
Characteristic Subtotal	
Digital Security Overview Running Subtotal	

Security Agenda Item: Entitlement Management

21. Are the following security solutions currently deployed or is deployment planned?

Address all:

a) ☐ Secure e-mail.	Deployed *(0.25)*	Planned *(0. 00)*	Neither *(0. 00)*.
b) ☐ PKI/Digital Certificates.	Deployed *(0.25)*	Planned *(0. 00)*	Neither *(0. 00)*.
c) ☐ Centralized User Authentication/ Authorisation/Policy Management.	Deployed *(0.25)*	Planned *(0. 00)*	Neither *(0. 00)*.
d) ☐ Single Sign-On (SSO).	Deployed *(0.25)*	Planned *(0. 00)*	Neither *(0. 00)*.
e) ☐ Web access control/ authorisation.	Deployed *(0.25)*	Planned *(0. 00)*	Neither *(0. 00)*.
f) ☐ Enterprise Directory Service.	Deployed *(0.25)*	Planned *(0. 00)*	Neither *(0. 00)*.
g) ☐ Smartcards/tokens.	Deployed *(0.25)*	Planned *(0. 00)*	Neither *(0. 00)*.
h) ☐ Biometrics.	Deployed *(0.25)*	Planned *(0. 00)*	Neither *(0. 00)*.
i) ☐ Remote access security.	Deployed *(0.25)*	Planned *(0. 00)*	Neither *(0. 00)*.
j) ☐ Wireless security.	Deployed *(0.25)*	Planned *(0. 00)*	Neither *(0. 00)*.
k) ☐ Enterprise Security Management.	Deployed *(0.25)*	Planned *(0. 00)*	Neither *(0. 00)*.
l) ☐ Security monitoring tools.	Deployed *(0.25)*	Planned *(0. 00)*	Neither *(0. 00)*.
m) ☐ Intrusion Detection systems.	Deployed *(0.25)*	Planned *(0. 00)*	Neither *(0. 00)*.

(Add all values to ascertain score.)	Agenda Item	Characteristic: (None)
Score		

22. Approximately what percentage of your IT support staff's efforts are related to user account/password management?

a) 1–5%.	1.75	
b) 5–15%.	1.00	
c) 15–25%.	0.50	
d) More than 25%.	0.00	
e) Do not know.	0.00	

	Agenda Item	Characteristic: (None)
Score		

Entitlement Management Subtotal	
Characteristic Subtotal	
Digital Security Overview Running Subtotal	

Security Agenda Item: Vulnerability Management

23. Which of the following statements best describes how vulnerabilities of critical systems are communicated to system administrators/security administrators?

a) The security administrators e-mail daily vulnerabilities to all IT personnel and it is the individual's responsibility to patch the systems.		1.00
b) The organisation separates groups by operating system groups whose responsibility it is to disseminate vulnerability information to the operating system group.		0.75
c) It is the responsibility of every system administrator to research and patch his or her own system(s).		0.50
d) We have no communication mechanism in place to alert administrators to vulnerabilities.		0.00
e) Other.		0.00
	Agenda Item	**Characteristic: (Enterprise-wide)**
Score		

24. How often does your organisation assess for known vulnerabilities?

a) Daily.	2.00	
b) Weekly.	1.50	
c) Monthly.	1.00	
d) Quarterly.	0.50	
e) Annually.	0.00	
f) Don't know.	0.00	
	Agenda Item	**Characteristic: (Continuous)**
Score		

25. In your opinion, which one of the following statements would best describe how effectively your organisation manages system vulnerabilities?

a) We have the ability to identify and track vulnerabilities as well as measure compliance.		2.00
b) We have wide-scale deployment of vulnerability tracking and knowledge of all critical infrastructure vulnerabilities.		1.50
c) Vulnerability information is obtained from various sources and administered on a periodic basis.		1.00
d) Vulnerability management is ad hoc and handled by IT or security staff alone.		0.50
e) Vulnerability management has not been addressed.		0.00
	Agenda Item	**Characteristic: (Proactive)**
Score		

Vulnerability Management Subtotal	
Characteristic Subtotal	
Digital Security Overview Running Subtotal	

Security Agenda Item: Business Continuity

26. In your opinion, which one of the following statements best describes your company's current business continuity/disaster recovery status?

a) No documented plans are in place.		0.00
b) Plans have been developed for recovering our mission-critical systems and data only.		0.25
c) Plans have been developed for recovering critical business processes only.		0.50
d) Plans have been developed for recovering mission-critical systems and some critical business processes.		0.75
e) Integrated plans have been developed for recovering the entire enterprise.		1.00
	Agenda Item	**Characteristic: (Formal)**
Score		

27. Over the past 12 months, what would you estimate are the number of downtime hours directly related to a disruption?

a) Less than 6 hours. 1.00		
b) 6–12 hours. 0.75		
c) 12–24 hours. 0.50		
d) 24–72 hours. 0.25		
e) More than 72 hours. 0.00		
	Agenda Item	**Characteristic: (Proactive)**
Score		

28. When was the last time you tested your business continuity/disaster recovery plans?

a) Within the last 6 months. 2.00		
b) Within the last year. 1.50		
c) Within the last 1–2 years. 1.00		
d) More than 3 years. 0.50		
e) Never been tested. 0.00		
	Agenda Item	**Characteristic: (Validated)**
Score		

29. Typically, what is the PRIMARY means of ensuring that your business continuity/disaster recovery plans are current?

a) Annual audit.	1.00	
b) Occasional spot checks.	0.75	
c) Updates are made following an incident.	0.50	
d) Updating is outsourced to a third party.	0.25	
e) No method in place.	0.00	
	Agenda Item	**Characteristic: (None)**
Score		

Business Continuity Subtotal	
Characteristic Subtotal	
Digital Security Overview Running Subtotal	

Agenda Item Grand Total (Max 45)	
Characteristic Grand Total (Max 30)	
Digital Security Overview Grand Total (Max 75)	

TABLE C.1   Scoring Matrix for an Effective Security Programme

	Aligned	Enterprise-wide	Continuous	Proactive	Validated	Formal	Totals: Agenda Items
Intrusion and Virus Detection							
Incident Response							
Privacy							
Policies, Standards, and Guidelines							
Physical Security							
Asset and Service Management							
Entitlement Management							
Vulnerability Management							
Business Continuity							
Totals: Characteristics							

Endnotes

Chapter 1   Living at the Digital Frontier

1. 2003 CSI/FBI Computer Crime and Security Survey.
2. *Ibid.*
3. *Ibid.*
4. 2004 DTI Information Security Breaches Survey.
5. *Ibid.*
6. *Ibid.*
7. Information Systems Audit and Control Foundation (ISAFC), *Board Briefing on IT Governance*. Available from www.itgi.org/boardbriefing.pdf
8. *Ibid.*
9. *Ibid.*
10. 2003 CSI/FBI Computer Crime and Security Survey.

Chapter 2   Security Characteristics

All text boxes in Chapter 2 are from the Ernst & Young 2004 Digital Security Survey. The full text of this document is Appendix C in this book.
1. For further information please see www.sarbanes-oxley.com.

Chapter 4   The Security Agenda

1. *The Security Agenda*®.
2. Ernst & Young, LLP, Policies, Standards and Guidelines 2002.
3. 2003 CSI/FBI Computer Crime and Security Survey.
4. Ernst & Young, LLP, 2002, Business Continuity.

Chapter 6   The Security Culture

1. For further information, please see www.sarbanes-oxley.com.

Chapter 7   The Risk Frontier

1. For further information, please see www.isfsecuritystandard.com.
2. For further information, please see www.isaca.org.
3. For further information, please see www.itil.com.
4. For further information, please see www.iso17799software.com.
5. For further information, please see www.sei.cmu.edu.

Appendix C   Ernst & Young 2004 Digital Security Overview

1. For further information please see Appendix C in the first edition of *Defending the Digital Frontier.*
2. Taken from a Symantec press release, 22 September 2003.

Glossary of Digital Security Terminology

3G A short term for third-generation wireless, and refers to near-future developments in personal and business wireless technology, especially mobile communications. This phase is expected to reach maturity over the next few years.

ADMINISTRATION The management of authentication credentials and authorisation privileges.

ALERT A message, triggered by an auditing or monitoring program, that describes a circumstance related to network security.

ANKLE-BITER A person with limited computer-related ability and/or knowledge who aspires to be a hacker or cracker.

ANOMALY DETECTION MODEL An intrusion detection model that looks for activity that differs from the normal user/system behaviour.

ANONYMOUS FTP A data retrieval system for File Transfer Protocol (FTP) servers that allows access to files by using the user ID *anonymous* instead of the more traditional user ID and password identifiers.

ANTIVIRUS PROGRAMS Utilities that search hard disks for viruses and remove any that are found. Most antivirus programs include an auto-update feature that enables the program to download profiles of new viruses so the application can check for the new viruses soon after discovery.

APPLICATION-LEVEL GATEWAY (FIREWALL) A protective network system configuration that maintains connections and redirects outgoing traffic so that the identity of the internal host server is replaced with the identity of the firewall.

ATTACK An attempt to bypass security controls on a system, or the exploitation of one or more vulnerabilities to cause harm to the target system.

AUDITING Conducting activities to assess the effectiveness of the people, processes, and technology that make up the digital security programme. Assessments are conducted to ensure that policy, procedures, and standards are implemented and followed, testing the effectiveness of the digital security programme.

AUTHENTICATION Procedures that involve establishing identity through three factors: knowledge (something that you *know*, for example, a password), possession (something that you *have*, for example, a random password generator or smart card), and identification (something that you *are*, for example, fingerprints or a retinal scan).

AUTHORISATION Procedures that involve assigning permissions to access specific digital assets.

AVAILABILITY The assumption that protected data will remain accessible on demand by authorised users.

BACK DOOR A feature frequently built into systems, programs, or applications that enables developers to have access for the purpose of fixing defects. These intentional vulnerabilities are also known as *trap doors*, and they are frequently exploited by hackers.

BACK ORIFICE A program that was developed as a remote administration tool. When installed on a computer or system, it enables a user (or hacker) to attain full system administrator privileges, including the ability to find passwords and confidential data and e-mail them out of the system.

BANDWIDTH The amount of data that can travel through a given medium.

BIOMETRICS The applied use of digital techniques to authenticate an authorised user's identity by verifying unique physical characteristics, such as fingerprints, voice, or retina.

BLENDED ATTACK Malicious code that uses multiple methods to spread.

BROADCAST STORM A network packet or series of packets sent through a gateway to communicate with all subnetworks. It initiates a reply from each system on the subnetworks with the goal of saturating the network and causing service outages. Also referred to as a *kamikaze packet* or *Chernobyl packet*.

BRUTE FORCE ATTACK An attack in which a system is inundated with every possible key or password until the correct one is entered.

BUFFER OVERFLOW The result of too much data being sent to a buffer or holding area in a script or software program. This is generally caused by poor software design or lazy software developers who neglect to properly handle too much or unexpected data as input to a program. This event can cause system crashes and also introduce back door vulnerabilities into a system.

BUG An unintentional flaw or vulnerability in a program or system that causes unwanted or unintended behaviours to occur.

CARNIVORE A system recently developed by the FBI for monitoring e-mail and other Internet traffic.

CENTRALISED LOGGING A function that enables systems administrators to forward messages from servers to a central system where they can be monitored more effectively. This allows the administrator to maintain a central archive of system logs and proactively scan for errors on systems throughout the network.

COMMON GATEWAY INTERFACE (CGI) A commonly used Web interface that enables servers, clients, operating systems, and programs to talk to each other.

CGI SCRIPTS Strings of code that enable the creation of interactive Web pages. These scripts can be a vulnerability for a Web server, particularly if the system security is porous.

CIPHERTEXT Encrypted data.

CONFIDENTIALITY The assumption that data in any state or location is protected from compromise.

CONTENT FILTERING A procedure for limiting access to undesirable or inappropriate Internet content. Content can be filtered or blocked based on traffic profiles or by site through the use of catalogued URLs.

CONTENT SCANNING A configurable security measure that captures malicious e-mail messages and/or attachments before they enter or leave the organisation's systems.

COOKIE A block of text placed on a hard drive by a Web site's server. Cookies contain information that assists the server to identify the user's computer. For example, the cookie placed on a user's computer by a Web site that requires a login may enable the user to bypass having to login every time he or she visits the Web site.

COUNTERMEASURE An action, tool, method, or technique that reduces an information system's vulnerability.

CRACK A tool that enables the user to decode encrypted passwords. It is used by system administrators to discern password-related vulnerabilities, but is more frequently used by hackers.

CRACKER A person who attempts to gain unauthorised access to computer systems with malicious intent.

CRASH The sudden failure of a computer system.

CRITICAL INFORMATION ASSETS Data upon which the organisation relies to conduct routine business, for instance, to generate revenue and facilitate communications or transactions. This definition incorporates sensitive and nonsensitive information.

CRITICAL NATIONAL INFRASTRUCTURE Physical or cyber-based system essential to the minimum operations of the economy and government.

CROSS-SITE SCRIPTING (XSS) The use of some of the functionality of active scripting against the user by inserting malicious code into the HTML that runs code on the user's computer, redirects him or her to a site other than the intended one, or steals passwords and personal information, among other things.

CYBERSPACE The system of globally-interconnected computers and communication systems.

CYBERWAR Information warfare.

DATA-DRIVEN ATTACK An attack in which seemingly benign data is allowed through a firewall and then executed by a user or an action.

DECRYPT To return encrypted data to its original or otherwise comprehensible form.

DEFAULT PASSWORD A password on a system when it is first delivered or installed.

DEMON DIALER A program that calls the same telephone number repeatedly.

DENIAL-OF-SERVICE ATTACK An orchestrated effort to deny service to an authorised user by overtaxing the resources of the system, thereby rendering it unable to respond to requests.

DIGITAL ASSET Information stored or processed by digital media or devices and the corresponding physical and logical devices used for storage, processing, or transport.

DIGITAL FRONTIER The forward edge of technological impact with respect to organisations' usage of technology and their reliance upon it for day-to-day operations to achieve marketable productivity improvements.

DIGITAL SECURITY GAP The vulnerabilities caused by the exuberant spending in the 1990s on upgraded and open-architecture technologies without commensurate spending on digital security.

DOMAIN NAME The title or name of an Internet host.

DROPPER A file used to conceal and transport a virus into a system or hard drive.

ENCRYPT To change the appearance of a message or data by assigning it a code in order to conceal its meaning from unauthorised persons.

FABRICATION Malicious and deliberate addition of false information into an information system.

FALSE NEGATIVE The indication by a system's security program that no intrusion has taken place when an intrusion actually has occurred.

FALSE POSITIVE The indication by a system's security program that an anomaly or intrusion has taken place when the noted behaviour is actually legitimate.

FIREWALL An electronic gate-keeping system that establishes a boundary between systems or networks for the purpose of limiting access and/or traffic.

FULCRUM OF CONTROL The point at which control and containment of a digital security incident becomes critical to the future of the organisation. Beyond this point, the situation may be impossible for the digital security team to control.

GATEWAY SCANNING A virus-scanning function implemented at the Internet gateway, enabling the system to contain a virus before it enters the network, and thereby minimising damage to business critical systems.

HACKER A person who attempts to gain unauthorised access to computer systems.

HACKING The attempt to gain unauthorised access to computer systems, whether successful or not.

HIGH-AVAILABILITY SYSTEM A system that has had technology applied or architecture adjusted to enable the system to operate at a higher level of robustness or to enable the end user of the system to maintain access or recover access to the information in the system in spite of otherwise debilitating events.

HIJACKING The interception of an active session by an unauthorised user. This can occur locally, for instance, if a user leaves his or her computer unsecured and connected. It can occur across a network or the Internet.

HOLE A system vulnerability that enables security countermeasures to be bypassed.

IN THE WILD Outside of a laboratory. This term is used to describe viruses or other malicious code. A virus laboratory is frequently referred to as a zoo.

INFORMATION ASSET Information possessed, whether through ownership or custodianship, by an organisation during the process of conducting business.

INFORMATION LIFECYCLE MANAGEMENT The principle of managing the entirety of an enterprise's data throughout its useful life.

INTEGRITY The assumption that data in any state or location is protected from unauthorised modification or deletion.

INTERCEPTION Malicious and deliberate capture of digital data in transit between systems or users.

INTERNET SERVICE PROVIDER (ISP) A company that provides Internet access to users.

INTERRUPTION Malicious and deliberate interference in electronic communications that renders networks, Web sites, or other electronic systems unusable.

INTRANET A private, internal company network.

INTRUSION DETECTION SYSTEM An Intrusion Detection System (IDS) gathers and analyses information from various areas within a computer or a network to identify possible security breaches, which include both intrusions (attacks from outside the organisation) and misuse (attacks from within the organisation).

INTRUSION PREVENTION SYSTEM Used to actively drop packets of data or disconnect connections that contain unauthorised data. Intrusion prevention technology is also commonly an extension of intrusion detection technology.

IP SECURITY (IPSEC) A security protocol from the Internet Engineering Task Force (IETF) that provides authentication and encryption over the Internet.

IP SPOOFING An attack in which a system uses another system's Internet protocol (IP) address without authorisation or for illicit means.

IT GOVERNANCE The oversight and guidance of information and applied technology within a business and business-related fields by stakeholders, which can include an organisation's directors and senior management, as well as process owners and IT suppliers, users, and auditors.

KEY PERFORMANCE INDICATORS (KPIs) Data sets against which a project or a company can benchmark its performance.

KEYSTROKE MONITORING The use of specialised software or a device to record every key struck by a computer user, and the computer's response.

LEAPFROG ATTACK The use of a password or user ID obtained in one attack to perpetrate another.

LETTER BOMB An e-mail message that contains malicious code that is activated when the message is opened.

LOGIC BOMB Software that performs a malicious or destructive action when specific conditions are met. Also called a *fork bomb* or *time bomb*.

LOW AND SLOW A general technique that applies to hackers that conceal or restrict their activities in an attempt to avoid detection by digital security countermeasures. The origin of this term is related to military operations that attempt to avoid detection by the enemy.

MAIL BOMB A large e-mail message or a large volume of e-mail messages that are sent to a user with the intent of crashing the recipient's system.

MALICIOUS CODE Software that is designed to damage a system, application, or data.

MALWARE A term used to describe any malicious software.

MAN IN THE MIDDLE A form of active wiretapping attack in which the attacker intercepts and selectively modifies communicated data in order to masquerade as one or more of the entities involved in a communication association.

MOCKINGBIRD An application that imitates a legitimate system feature or function but engages in malicious behaviours when activated.

MODIFICATION Malicious and deliberate changes to access controls to allow unauthorised privileges or to deny authorised privileges.

NETWORK Two or more computers interconnected to enable communications.

NONREPUDIATION An administrative method of verifying delivery of a message in which both the sender and recipient are verified.

PASSWORD SNIFFING Analyzing network traffic to discern passwords.

PAYLOAD The action performed during a virus attack.

PERIMETER-BASED SECURITY Applying access controls to all entry and exit points on a network for the purpose of securing it.

PHISHING (sometimes called *carding* or *brand spoofing*) A scam where the perpetrator sends out legitimate-looking e-mails appearing to come from some of the Web's biggest sites, including eBay, PayPal, MSN, Yahoo!, BestBuy, and America Online, in an effort to phish (pronounced "fish") for personal and financial information from the recipient.

PHREAKING Breaking into a telephone network with malicious or mischievous intent.

PIGGYBACK To gain unauthorised access to a computer system by using an authorised user's legitimate connection.

PING (PACKET INTERNET GROUPER) A program that sends test packets to a destination system to ascertain if the system is live.

PING OF DEATH The use of an extremely large ping packet with the intention of causing a denial-of-service attack.

PRIVACY The right of an individual to determine to what degree he or she is willing to disclose personal or other information. When such information is provided to other entities, individuals, or organisations, this right extends to the collection, distribution, and storage of that information.

PROXY A tool that substitutes its own IP address for that of the address of the protected network as traffic passes through a firewall.

REPLICATOR A program that can produce copies of itself.

REVERSE PROXY A gateway for servers, one which enables a Web server to provide content from another one transparently. As with a standard proxy, a reverse proxy may serve to improve performance of the Web by caching; this is a simple way to mirror a Web site. But the most common reason to run a reverse proxy is to enable controlled access from the Web at large to servers behind a firewall.

RISK POSTURE The level of organisational security as aligned with the five threat categories described in Chapter 8. It is the curve that signifies the theoretical capabilities of the organisation to mitigate risk (up and to the right of the curve) and the theoretical risk that an organisation is accepting (down and to the left) by choosing to take the chance that those incidents will not occur or have impacts that are within the limits of tolerance.

RISK PROFILE The organisation's risk with regard to digital security and its business objectives.

ROOTKIT A tool that provides a back door into systems for legitimate and illegitimate information-gathering purposes, as well as many other clandestine purposes.

SAMURAI An electronic locksmith or legitimate hacker who performs legal, research-oriented snooping for clients.

SECURITY ADMINISTRATOR TOOL FOR ANALYZING NETWORKS (SATAN) A tool for identifying network system security weaknesses and vulnerabilities remotely.

SCRIPT KIDDIE A person of limited technical knowledge and ability who employs automated tools and exploits known vulnerabilities to disrupt networked systems.

SECURITY FRONTIER The organisation's security risk (probability and potential impact of failure) superimposed on productivity (an organisation's usage of and reliance on technology).

SECURITY MANAGEMENT GAP The distance between the top levels of management and the security team, which is also the distance between the organisation's business goals and the IT department's protection of those goals.

SECURE SHELL (SSH) Sometimes known as Secure Socket Shell, it is a Unix-based command interface and protocol for securely getting access to a remote computer. It is widely used by network administrators to control Web and other kinds of servers remotely.

SECURITY RISK The proportionally increased risk a company faces in relation to its proximity to the edge of the digital frontier, based on the higher probability of failure of systems relied upon and the increased impact of that failure when it occurs.

SENSITIVE INFORMATION ASSETS Data, physical or digital, that could, if compromised, pose grave threats to the organisation.

SIMPLE MAIL TRANSPORT PROTOCOL (SMTP) The delivery format used by Internet e-mail for transmitting messages between servers.

SMART CARD An access card that contains information that can identify the user.

SMURFING A form of a denial-of-service attack in which the attackers message impersonates (spoofs) the source address of a ping packet to a network's broadcast address. This contrived ping causes all the network machines to respond simultaneously to the unsuspecting victim network, clogging and potentially crashing the network.

SNARF The act of taking a large document or file with intent to use it with or without the author's permission.

SNEAKER A security expert or legitimate hacker who is hired to test systems' security by breaking into them.

SNIFFER A network monitoring program that captures data as it crosses a network. Network and systems administrators use sniffers for legitimate purposes, such as troubleshooting. Hackers and others use sniffers to steal user IDs and passwords.

SOCIAL ENGINEERING Techniques used by hackers and virus developers to activate viruses or to glean information from unsuspecting computer users.

SPAM Excessive amounts of information sent to a user or a site with the intention of causing the system to crash.

SPOOFING The practice of assuming the identity of another user, for example, by using someone else's password or email account.

SECURE SOCKETS LAYER (SSL) An authentication and confidentiality protocol for software applications.

SUBVERSION Modification of intrusion detection operations by an intruder to force the system to produce false negatives.

TERMINAL HIJACKING An attacker takes control of another user's terminal session in progress on a specific machine and is able to send and receive information while that user is on the terminal.

THREAT TO AN INFORMATION SYSTEM Any potential act upon or against the system, of internal or external origin, that is performed with the intention to cause harm.

Tiger Teams Groups of computer experts, frequently comprising government or industry experts, that seek out vulnerabilities by testing system defences.

Tiger A software tool that scans a system and looks for vulnerabilities.

Time Bomb A software program that requires an action, frequently malicious, to occur at a specific time or on a specific date, or if some specific event occurs or does not occur. An example would be that if the author of the program is fired and therefore does not log in for a certain number of days, files would be deleted or a virus would be triggered.

Tinkerbell Program A monitoring program that scans network entry points and alerts system security when traffic from specific sites commences, or when specific login IDs are used.

Trace Packet A unique packet used in a packet-switching network. The packet issues progress reports to the network control centre as it moves through a system.

Traceroute An information-gathering operation that traces the route of UDP probe packets between the local and remote hosts.

Triggered Event A behaviour or action caused by malicious code, such as a virus, when certain conditions exist or have been met. An example of a triggered event would be the deletion of all files in a computer's root directory ("C drive") on a certain date or after a specific application has been launched. Also called *sleeper programs*.

Tripwire A software tool used with databases that notifies systems administrators when files' byte count changes.

Trojan Horse Program A nonreplicating, malicious software program that appears to be benign but which enables unauthorised access to information systems without the user's knowledge.

Tunneling A procedure that viruses use to prevent antivirus software from detecting malicious code.

Two-Factor Authentication Use of two different elements to authenticate a user, such as a password and a token. See *authentication*.

Vaccine A program that performs a signature check on executable files and alerts system administrators if changes have been made.

VAPORWARE Software that is still in the conceptual or design phase.

VIRTUAL PRIVATE NETWORK (VPN) A way to use a public telecommunication infrastructure, such as the Internet, to provide remote offices or individual users with secure access to their organisation's network.

VIRUS A self-replicating computer program file that can attach itself to other files or disks and modify them, usually without a user's permission or knowledge. Many viruses, though not all, inflict damage. A partial list of virus types appears below.

- **ANTI-ANTIVIRUS VIRUS** A virus that targets antivirus software.
- **ANTIVIRUS VIRUS** A virus that detects and disables other viruses.
- **ARMORED VIRUS** A virus that contains the capability to disassemble or reverse-engineer its code in order to prevent examination or detection.
- **CAVITY VIRUS** A virus that overwrites a part of the file in which it resides but does not alter the file's functionality or increase the size of the file, which enables it to evade detection.
- **CLUSTER VIRUS** A virus that modifies a computer in such a way that, after infection, launching any application will cause the virus to execute.
- **COMPANION VIRUS** A virus that mimics a system file with a similar name, but assigns itself a higher launch priority so that the virus will execute before the default program file.
- **RESIDENT VIRUS** A resident virus infiltrates a computer's memory and does not activate until a trigger event occurs.
- **RETROVIRUS** A virus that continues to infect a system until every backup system and all backup media are infected. The net result of this is that it is not possible to cleanse and restore the system.
- **SELF-ENCRYPTING VIRUS** A virus that encrypts its code differently for each infection in an attempt to avoid detection by antivirus software.
- **SELF-GARBLING VIRUS** A virus that attempts to deceive antivirus software by changing the way its code is structured.
- **SLOW INFECTOR VIRUS** A virus that only infects files when they are created or modified.
- **SPARSE VIRUS** A virus that avoids detection by infecting files only when certain conditions exist (such as file size) or have been met (such as a date that has passed).
- **STEALTH VIRUS** A type of virus that conceals itself from antivirus software by providing a clean but false version of the file the antivirus software is seeking.

VOICE OVER IP (VoIP) Voice delivered using the Internet Protocol is a term used in IP telephony for a set of facilities for managing the delivery of voice information using the Internet Protocol (IP). In general, this means sending voice information in digital form in discrete packets rather than in the traditional circuit-committed protocols of the public switched telephone network (PSTN).

VULNERABILITIES Inherent weaknesses in an information system, or weaknesses that are the result of deliberate acts or omissions.

WAR DIALER A software program that dials a range or a list of numbers for the purpose of detecting dial-in access to computer systems. The program records those numbers answering with an electronic handshake, which can indicate an entry point to a digital system.

WAR DRIVING The process of travelling around looking for wireless access point signals that can be used to get network access.

WAR CHALKING Process of marking areas, usually on pavements with chalk, that receive wireless signals that can be accessed.

WAR NIBBLING The process of mapping Bluetooth devices within an organisation.

WINDOWS PRODUCT ACTIVATION (WPA) The mandatory product registration system included in Microsoft's Windows XP, Office XP, and recent Office products (such as Word 2002 or Excel 2002) as a means of enforcing compliance with the company's End User License Agreement (EULA).

WORM An independent parasitic software program that replicates but does not infect other program files. A worm can replicate on the host computer and stay there, or replicate and send copies of itself to other machines on a network. The damage it inflicts is primarily a service overload that creates gridlock on networks and information systems that can be serious enough to force them to be shut down.

ZERO DAY A zero-day exploit is one that takes advantage of a security vulnerability on the same day that the vulnerability becomes generally known.

ZOO A group of viruses that have been collected for research purposes.

Index